The Cultural Revolution: A Very Short Introduction

VERY SHORT INTRODUCTIONS are for anyone wanting a stimulating and accessible way in to a new subject. They are written by experts and have been published in more than 25 languages worldwide.

The series began in 1995 and now represents a wide variety of topics in history, philosophy, religion, science, and the humanities. The VSI library now contains 300 volumes—a Very Short Introduction to everything from ancient Egypt and Indian philosophy to conceptual art and cosmology—and will continue to grow in a variety of disciplines.

Available soon:

For more information visit our website

www.oup.co.uk/general/vsi/

Richard Curt Kraus

THE CULTURAL REVOLUTION

A Very Short Introduction

OXFORD
UNIVERSITY PRESS

Oxford University Press, Inc., publishes works that further
Oxford University's objective of excellence
in research, scholarship, and education.

Oxford New York
Auckland Cape Town Dar es Salaam Hong Kong Karachi
Kuala Lumpur Madrid Melbourne Mexico City Nairobi
New Delhi Shanghai Taipei Toronto

With offices in
Argentina Austria Brazil Chile Czech Republic France Greece
Guatemala Hungary Italy Japan Poland Portugal Singapore
South Korea Switzerland Thailand Turkey Ukraine Vietnam

Published by Oxford University Press, Inc.
198 Madison Avenue, New York, NY 10016

www.oup.com

Oxford is a registered trademark of Oxford University Press

Library of Congress Cataloging-in-Publication Data
Kraus, Richard Curt.
The cultural revolution : a very short introduction / Richard Curt Kraus.
p. cm.
Includes bibliographical references and index.
ISBN 978-0-19-974055-0 (pbk.)
1. China—History—Cultural Revolution, 1966–1976. I. Title.
DS778.7.K73 2012
951.05'6—dc23   2011025599

Printed by Integrated Books International, United States of America
on acid-free paper

For Anthony Kraus, a civilized beast

Contents

List of illustrations

Preface

China's Great Proletarian Cultural Revolution shook the politics of China and the world between 1966 and 1976. It dominated every aspect of Chinese life: families were separated, careers upended, education interrupted, and striking political initiatives attempted amid a backdrop of chaos, new beginnings, and the settling of old scores.

Yet the movement remains contentious for its radicalism, its ambitious scale, and its impact upon almost a billion lives. It is difficult to make sense out of this complex, often obscure, and still painful period. This book attempts to offer a coherent narrative. Fortunately, we can now draw upon a vital literature of scholarship, memoirs, and popular culture, which has appeared both inside and outside China.

The Cultural Revolution was violent, yet it was also a source of inspiration and social experiment. Why did the Cultural Revolution exhilarate people, and why did so many become disillusioned? The challenge is to take the Cultural Revolution seriously rather than simply dismissing it for its absurdities and cruelties.

Much of what we think we know about the Cultural Revolution turns out to be mistaken. For example, most of the features of the Cultural Revolution were already in place nearly two years before its ostensible beginning in 1966. Red Guard membership was much more extensive than Westerners imagine, but the youth movement's heyday was much shorter, less than two years. Arts policy was destructive yet also part of a longer-term plan for modernizing China's culture. The Cultural Revolution shook the economy but certainly did not shatter it, for it grew at a respectable rate. Despite China's isolation, the Cultural Revolution laid the foundation for China's transformation into a manufacturing platform for a neoliberal world economy. The Cultural Revolution is far from forgotten in China today, nor does the government ban its discussion.

The story of the Cultural Revolution is complex. I try to minimize the specialized jargon that crops up in writing about Chinese politics, but readers should be warned about the odd word "cadre," a Party or state bureaucrat in the People's Republic. The word refers to individual officials, not to a group as in the West. I have tried to be sparing in introducing unfamiliar Chinese place names, although this may make the Cultural Revolution seem more Beijing-centered than is warranted; it was an intense national movement with many local peculiarities. Names of political campaigns also play a larger role than in Western public life. To Chinese, instead of mystification they offer a mnemonic tag and a context for both political and emotional assessments of the Cultural Revolution's diverse currents.

Chapter 1
Introduction: China's unfinished revolution

China's Great Proletarian Cultural Revolution sprang to life in May 1966 and lasted through the death of Mao Zedong in 1976. It was proletarian more in aspiration than in reality, given that four-fifths of Chinese were peasants. It was cultural, in that its most consistent targets were the arts and popular beliefs. It was not in itself a great revolution; it made a lot of noise but only shook up the state—it did not overturn it. Like most revolutions, it overstayed its welcome. It is tempting to regard this raucous decade as the last and perhaps final push in a century-long trajectory of Chinese revolution, after which China got down to the serious business of building a modern nation.

China's present leaders, often former Red Guards themselves, have little interest in examining the link between Maoist China and the country today. They avoid awkward discussions about their own youth, and they adhere to an unspoken understanding to discard recriminations from that period. Western media are tempted to sharpen the contrast between a good China (which fills our stores with products and carries our debt) and a bad China (which once marked the limit of Western power in the world). But accounts that simply proclaim Mao Zedong to be a crazy tyrant, and that China's *real* modern history begins only with his death, miss important dimensions of the rapid and penetrating social change that has occurred since the Cultural Revolution's end.

1. Map of China.

In contrast, this book draws out the connections between the isolated and beleaguered China of the 1960s and the newly risen global power of today. These two Chinas are not the opposites that we sometimes want them to be. Like other twentieth-century Chinese leaders, Mao wanted a strong, modern China; some Cultural Revolution policies contributed to this goal, others were remarkably unhelpful but even so added to the distinctive direction followed by contemporary China.

Rather than fence off the Cultural Revolution as a historical swamp, one can stress its connections to our present world, situating this rather nationalist Chinese movement within a global context. The Cultural Revolution was part of the global movement of radical youth in the 1960s and 1970s. Western protestors boasted of imagined or emotional links to China's rebels. During the Cultural Revolution Beijing and Washington tempered their long hostility with Nixon's 1971 visit, reshaping the international politics of Asia, and sowing seeds for China's decades of spectacular economic growth. The Cultural Revolution and its subsequent anti-leftist purge battered China's bureaucracy so severely that there was little cogent questioning of policies that turned the nation into a vast workhouse for the world's globalized industry.

Modernization and nationalism in China's revolutions

The iconoclastic revolutionary tradition of modern China begins at least with the failed Taiping Rebellion of the mid-nineteenth century, the bloodiest effort to overthrow the weak and corrupt Qing Dynasty, which finally fell in 1911. The Guomindang (Nationalist Party) of Sun Yat-sen and then Chiang Kai-shek gave revolution a more modern face in a sustained effort to unite and modernize China. They were joined by the Communists, first as allies, then as rivals in a civil war to determine how extreme the revolution would be. When the Guomindang retreated to Taiwan in 1949, the socialist revolution on the mainland was secured.

But the revolution in culture had only begun. Each of the revolutionary waves that swept over twentieth-century China was passionately concerned with transforming culture. Many would say that that Qing Dynasty's collapse was heralded by its abolition of the classical civil service examination in 1905, sundering a centuries-old nexus of education, upward mobility, social control, and ideological dominion.

In the confused decade following the 1911 establishment of the Chinese Republic, modernizing intellectuals led the May Fourth movement of 1919. Demonstrations on that date protested Japan's receiving Germany's former territorial privileges in China at the end of World War I, but May Fourth activists carried a much broader modernist agenda. Dominating China's intellectual life for decades, the May Fourth movement regarded the major obstacle to social progress and modernity to be Confucian culture with its patriarchy, land tenure system, and opposition to learning foreign ways. The May Fourth modernizers believed in the liberation promised by science, and in the transformative potential of democracy. They also claimed a special mission for intellectuals in leading China, a privileged position not so different from the Confucianism they opposed.

China's revolutionary politics were also nationalist as well as modernizing, punctuated by strikes, demonstrations, and boycotts against foreign firms, and finally overwhelmed by the enormity of Japan's invasion. Although critics charged May Fourth activists with Westernizing China away from its own roots, indignation at imperialism kept that from occurring. The Guomindang under Chiang Kai-shek organized a "New Life movement" to attack superstition, close temples, destroy statues of feudal gods, and urge a new morality for China, but then backed away from such radicalism.

5

The new Communist Party, profoundly influenced by the May Fourth movement, early emphasized cultural transformation. But after Mao Zedong's 1935 ascendency as Party leader culture occupied a new and central strategic role. Mao, one of the founders of the Communist Party in 1921, became the Party's chief by leading Communist rebels from their South China bases, surrounded by Guomindang forces, to the remote northwestern city of Yan'an, in 1934–35. This year-long strategic retreat, known as the Long March, preserved a core of the Communist troops but forced the Party to rethink its relationship to their local peasant hosts.

As the war with Japan intensified, Mao recognized that the Party needed to win the support and trust of China's peasants. The Party set up a program to retrain urban intellectuals and former workers to accomplish this. This 1942 rectification movement involved conscious rejection of elitist ways, a sometimes chest-thumping celebration of peasant virtues, and a series of arts productions aimed at spreading revolutionary values by appealing to peasant audiences. The Maoist rectification sharpened the Party's ability to combat both the Japanese invaders and the Guomindang. At the same time, it suppressed the cosmopolitan tendencies of May Fourth, preferring peasant art to imported music and drama. In 1945 the Communists adapted Chinese opera (*The White-Haired Girl*) and ballet from a well-known peasant dance (*yang-ge*), and it encouraged Party intellectuals to write in accessible, nonliterary ways.

The arts were intended to serve politics. But Mao also argued that higher artistic standards would create more persuasive propaganda. Most of the intellectuals at Yan'an went along with the new nativist line happily enough. They could see its effectiveness when peasant audiences viewing *The White-Haired Girl* wanted to kill the actor singing the role of the evil landlord. But after the Japanese defeat, and after the flight of the Guomindang, many of the Yan'an ways were put aside, as the victorious Red Army marched into China's cities, and the Communist Party assumed rule over a sophisticated nation, rather than a guerilla base in the hinterlands. The Party's cultural agenda broadened, readmitting some of the cosmopolitan instincts put aside at Yan'an. One Communist painter exclaimed excitedly on the eve of the liberation of Beijing: at last we will be able to make oil paintings!

The first seventeen years

Revolutionary China's first decade was broadly successful. The new People's Republic restored social order after a devastating civil war. Land reform and new economic programs brought dramatic economic growth. Military success against the United States in the Korean War encouraged new respect for Beijing. Expansion of higher education pleased intellectuals eager to build a better China, and the arts looked both to foreign and to native traditional inspiration.

The first important sign of indecision among Communist Party leaders came with the Hundred Flowers campaign of 1956–57. Overly confident in the wake of a smooth "Socialist Transformation" of economic life in 1956, Mao Zedong reached out to non-Party intellectuals, encouraging them to speak out on public affairs, even to criticize the Communist Party. At first hesitant, many intellectuals eventually responded to the appeal to "Let a Hundred Flowers Blossom," revealing greater bitterness than the Party had anticipated. Changing course abruptly, leaders abandoned the liberalism of the Hundred Flowers for a fierce anti-rightist campaign in 1957, in which a million intellectuals were labeled as "rightist elements," many losing their jobs and some sent to labor reform camps for the next two decades.

Silencing the critics encouraged the Great Leap Forward of 1958, a massive effort to break through constraints on economic growth by mobilizing China's greatest resource, its labor power. The Great Leap was visionary, exhilarating, and mistaken. Newly established agricultural cooperatives were combined into larger communes, aiming to gain productive power through reorganization, including pooling child care and cooking. While the Great Leap did bring important infrastructural changes in the form of new agricultural factories, roads, and bridges, a lack of administrative feedback exacerbated unrealistic production goals. Lower officials, anxious of being judged "rightist," too quickly assured their bosses of successes in every field. The Party emphasized the contributions that could be made by politically inspired amateurs, denigrating the constraints often posed by professional experts. There were huge public works projects, some of which were successful, and other campaigns that were ultimately harebrained, such as the poorly conceived "backyard" steel smelters or the campaign to destroy sparrows.

The Great Leap resulted in a vast famine as agricultural production collapsed in many provinces. Operating with unfoundedly optimistic production figures, the state increased quotas for grain procurement even as it reduced resources for agricultural production. Disease and malnutrition resulted in perhaps twenty million to thirty million deaths in 1960–61, the greatest famine of the twentieth century.

The Party was slow in comprehending this disaster. Aware that the Great Leap was not going well, in the spring of 1959 Mao withdrew as head of state in favor of Liu Shaoqi, veteran leader of the Communist underground during the revolution. Later that year, several senior Party leaders faulted the Great Leap for being poorly administered, overly ambitious, and out of touch with the people. Marshal Peng Dehuai, the minister of defense and a veteran revolutionary, led the criticism. Mao's response was fierce and unrelenting. The purge of Marshal Peng reminded all how strong a cult the Party had built around Mao Zedong, and how difficult it was to constrain him.

The economic emergency was exacerbated by the collapse of China's relations with the Soviet Union. Once China's "elder brother in socialism," Soviet leaders were suspicious of Chinese assertions of an autonomous developmental path. Past military cooperation in Korea faded when China sought help in building an atomic bomb. A Soviet bomb was readied for shipment to China, only to be held back as Soviet leaders hesitated to build up a potential rival. As conflict intensified, in 1960 the Soviets recalled six thousand technical advisors, who took with them the blueprints for hundreds of unfinished industrial projects, leaving their Chinese comrades in the lurch.

Tensions with the Soviet Union probably strengthened Mao's hand at a time of great vulnerability, by stoking Chinese nationalism. While Mao retained the Party chairmanship, China tried desperate experiments to repair economic damage from the Great Leap. Local leaders relaxed their Great Leap intolerance of profit-making peasant markets in order to stimulate food production. Supervision of cultural activities lightened, as the Party cultivated the intellectuals and experts whom it had recently punished.

Rekindling the fire of revolution

The political situation was tense as the Party sought to lead the nation beyond the "three bad years" of 1959, 1960, and 1961. Mao Zedong kept his position as Party chairman, although daily administration was in the hands of President Liu Shaoqi and the Party secretary-general Deng Xiaoping. Liu and Deng supported lightening the hand of the Party, mild market reforms, and a looser cultural regime, all within a familiar Leninist framework. Mao and his followers did not accept such liberalization easily, instead advocating greater political work to keep China from abandoning its revolution.

A fundamental principle of Chinese politics is that the political elite maintains an appearance of unity, even when disagreeing strongly. Thus tensions over policy choices were hidden. Indeed, the array of policy options under experimentation were not viewed as two diametrically opposed policy "lines" except retroactively, after the Cultural Revolution began. When the Cultural Revolution began in 1966, radicals criticized the "Seventeen Years" since the establishment of the People's Republic of China in 1949. Their goal was to make the case for a sharp departure from a period they misrepresented as a unity.

One area of contention was rural corruption. A "Socialist Education Campaign," launched in 1962, sought to boost fading revolutionary spirit within the Party by emphasizing ideological purity and recalling the class struggles that had brought the Communists to power. Disagreement over Maoist approaches to handling local leadership in the countryside elicited resistance from Liu Shaoqi, Deng Xiaoping, and other top leaders.

Despairing that administrative campaigns would ever shake up the bureaucracy, Mao lectured his colleagues in 1962 that they should "never forget class struggle." This meant talking about it "every year, every month, every day, at conferences, at party congresses, at plenary sessions, and at each and every meeting." Mao hoped to reinvigorate the Chinese revolution by calling upon people to be true to its historical roots in overthrowing capitalists and landlords, and to protect the new status of workers and peasants.

Mao pressed for a revolution within the revolution. In the chairman's view, the old ruling classes had been overthrown shortly after the establishment of the People's Republic in 1949, yet their influence lived on in people's everyday assumptions and behavior. The revolution had destroyed the material bases for landlord and capitalist power, but their ideologies were embedded within new China's institutions, especially education, the arts, and popular culture. Mao distinguished between two kinds of counterrevolutionary influence. Feudalism, the product of the old landlord class, was often at odds with the bourgeois ideology adapted by Chinese capitalists, heavily influenced by their foreign ties. However, in defeat, the two defeated social forces joined hands to confuse and mislead Communists, discouraging their proper ambitions and deflecting them from their goals.

Thus one did not have to be an actual property holder to hold capitalist or landlord beliefs. Indeed, one of the Cultural Revolution's most common terms of abuse would become "capitalist roader," applied to veteran Communists who strayed from the Maoist path. Mao's approach was strikingly nonmaterial for a lifelong Marxist, but it represented his effort to come to grips with the new dynamics of socialist China. And it provided an intellectual foundation for a massive purge of his enemies in the Party.

After the revolution, the Party oscillated between left-leaning periods, when the virtues of workers, peasants, and soldiers were paramount, and conservative phases when the "masses of laboring people" was a more inclusive concept, extending to intellectuals, office workers, shopkeepers, and other such classically "petty bourgeois" citizens. The call to remember class struggle signaled Mao's leftism at a time when his Party rivals were tolerating or encouraging much more eclectic economic policies. The Maoist ideal of a Party for workers, peasants, and soldiers was counterpoised against the notion of a Party that reached out also to intellectuals, technical experts, religious leaders, overseas Chinese, and former capitalists.

These strains were barely contained in the four years leading up the Cultural Revolution. Mao Zedong was honored by all in name, but he complained that the Party secretary-general Deng Xiaoping treated him like the corpse at a funeral, respecting his image but ignoring his views. Others were more supportive, especially the new minister of defense, Marshal Lin Biao. Lin, one of the heroes of the revolution, replaced Mao's critic, Marshal Peng Dehuai. He led a program to expand the army's prominence and political impact. When China exploded a nuclear bomb in 1964, the prestige of the military increased. Lin molded the army into a bastion of leftist politics. He halted trends toward professionalization of the officer corps by abolishing titles of military rank and their insignia. China's army was made up of peasant recruits, and the Ministry of Defense regarded itself in some measure as the political patron and even voice of millions of peasants. Mao turned also to a group of radical intellectuals, and increasingly, to his wife, Jiang Qing.

Jiang Qing's 1938 marriage to Mao in Yan'an had provoked controversy among top Party leaders. Many remained fond of Mao's previous wife and distrusted the Shanghai actress who had beguiled their leader. They compelled the new couple to agree that Jiang Qing would stand back from political leadership. Jiang Qing accepted this begrudgingly, taking low-level assignments in cultural organizations in the 1950s. But by the early 1960s she was restive, resentful, and a willing ally for her increasingly angry husband. As tensions mounted in 1966, she linked up with Lin Biao to organize a February conference on the arts within the People's Liberation Army, marking both her new public role and underscoring that the army was in Mao's camp.

From 1962 through 1966, Mao and his followers organized many model programs that later became identified with the Cultural Revolution. Mao's "Little Red Book" (*Quotations from the Works of Mao Zedong*) was prepared by the army in 1963 to spread radical values among soldiers through required political study. Urban young people began to be resettled in the countryside in a serious program that would be adapted to rid cities of troublesome Red Guards by 1968. Maoist canonization of the model soldier, Lei Feng, began 1963. The Dazhai production brigade, the Maoist model for rural organization, established its political credentials in 1964, as did its twin model for industry, the Daqing oil field. The Third Front economic development campaign, by which new industries were built in secure interior regions, was launched in 1964, albeit with secrecy.

That does not mean to suggest that the Cultural Revolution really began several years earlier than we know. But Mao and his supporters already had a coherent program for China. The eruption of political turbulence after 1966 was fueled in part by their frustrations in carrying out these leftward initiatives against the resistance of a professional bureaucratic elite, which was busy developing a more stable and routinized system. What Mao added in 1966 to fire up the Cultural Revolution was the mass mobilization of groups who had not previously been active in Chinese politics.

Mao, feeling that the Party organization was controlled by his adversaries, and fearful of his rivals, turned beyond the Party for allies. Just as he recruited new leaders for his cause, he turned to non-Party activists, the "rebels" who answered his call for "a Great Proletarian Cultural Revolution." Mao's appeals struck a chord with many who felt that life in China was unfair, that it had not lived up to ideals of revolution.

Mao Zedong met with the visiting novelist and French minister of culture André Malraux, in 1965. Mao told Malraux that "the thought, culture, and customs which brought China to where we found her must disappear, and the thought, customs, and culture of proletarian China, which does not yet exist, must appear." Mao also believed that the attainment of Communism was a serious issue, not an abstract theoretical quest. He mockingly dismissed the Soviet premier, Andrei Kosygin, for saying that "'Communism means the raising of living standards.' Of course! And swimming is a way of putting on a pair of trunks!"

The rise and fall of the Cultural Revolution, a drama in two acts

Although the eleven years of Cultural Revolution are typically treated as a coherent era, we can better understand it as divided into two very different phases. The movement exploded with a sudden and intense burst of radicalism by Red Guards, frustrated workers, and ambitious junior officials in 1966–67. This mass mobilization phase of the Cultural Revolution succeeded in driving Mao's rivals from power. The second phase of the Cultural Revolution lasted from 1968 to 1976 and consolidated a new Maoist order by negotiations and force to bring rebel groups under control. Revolution was thus followed by repression, as a reconstituted Party suppressed the rebels of 1966. This second period was punctuated in 1971 by the violent death of Mao's anointed successor, Lin Biao. This scandal unsettled most Chinese, leading the movement to drag on as an ailing Chairman Mao presided distantly and ineffectually over factional infighting until his death in 1976.

I. Radical Fervor: 1966–67

The Cultural Revolution erupted when Chairman Mao felt shut out by more conservative comrades, and fought to re-impose his influence. The Great Proletarian Cultural Revolution was officially initiated in May 1966 and was different from all of the campaigns of the previous seventeen years because it was directed against the Communist Party-state itself.

As Mao prepared for the Cultural Revolution, he found that Beijing was under the control of his adversaries. He turned to China's second great city, Shanghai, for political support. There, Maoist writers found an outlet for articles that no one in the capital would publish, and several talented and ambitious local figures aligned themselves to the Maoist cause.

At Mao's behest, the Shanghai writer Yao Wenyuan wrote a critique of a 1961 drama *Hai Rui Dismissed from Office*. Although set in the Ming dynasty, this play could be read allegorically, as a defense of Marshal Peng Dehuai for daring to criticize Mao Zedong over the Great Leap. The author of the drama, Wu Han, was no political novice but a vice-mayor of Beijing. Mao's strategy was to isolate conservative Party leaders by attacking their underlings. Thus when Beijing Party boss Peng Zhen was unable to halt the criticism of Wu Han and shield this member of his political entourage, he fell from power himself. With the Beijing Party office in chaos, Mao could more easily attack Liu Shaoqi and Deng Xiaoping.

As Mao pushed to put right his Party, he overcame resistance by enlisting new allies from outside normal political life. By enlarging the realm of political participation, Mao turned especially to students. They responded by forming spontaneous organizations of "Red Guards," eager to confront teachers, local party leaders, and almost anyone in authority. In an authoritarian society where occasions to speak out were few, Mao encouraged the teens to attack his enemies. Red Guards quickly organized mass meetings, published newspapers, posted "big-character posters" in public spaces, raided homes of imagined enemies. and even set up prisons for overthrown officials. Their youth and lack of social responsibilities not only fueled their activism but also encouraged internal divisions and reckless behavior.

As the existing Party organization was shattered, Maoists formed a new and ad hoc Central Cultural Revolution Group. It initially had a hard time establishing its authority beyond Beijing. A "January Storm" in Shanghai overthrew the old local Party organization, but radicals found it difficult to extend this model through the nation. Rival Red Guard organizations, often linked to different backers in the state and Party bureaucracy, warred with one another. Even Mao's supporters were shocked by the violence and anarchy. The public humiliation of once respected senior officials in mass criticism meetings unnerved many who had been allied with the Chairman. Some expressed their resistance in a series of meetings in early 1967, castigated as the "February Adverse Current." But they made their point. The army hesitated to intervene in disputes between competing groups claiming to uphold the true revolutionary line, but was inevitably drawn into the conflict. By early 1968, the army intervened to restore order with increasing frequency, especially in areas where Red Guard factions waged local civil war.

II. Establishing Revolutionary Order, 1968–76

Putting a cap on the wilder side of Cultural Revolutionary mass politics began in earnest in 1968. By then, the purge of conservative officials such as President Liu Shaoqi and other "capitalist roaders" was complete. But continuing conflicts among Red Guard and rebel organizations remained chaotic, disrupting the economy. Maoists also took notice of external pressures. To the north, military tensions with the Soviet Union increased, while to the south, the United States escalated its invasion of Vietnam.

The victorious Maoists took several measures to restore order. First, competing radical organizations were compelled to unite. Negotiating the reconstruction of local authority was complex, and the new political role of the army—Maoists with guns—was critical. The army backed the new "revolutionary committees," local administrative bodies that drew upon a "triple alliance" of rebel activists, leftist bureaucrats, and military commanders. Military leaders brokered the local arrangements, province by province, and typically held the greatest power. Second, the Red Guards were packed off to the countryside to do agricultural work as participants in the "Up to the Mountains, Down to the Villages" movement. Expanding this existing program cleared the political field by forcing the Red Guards to steel themselves by living and working with peasant activists. Third, a secretive campaign to "clean up class ranks" reviewed individual dossiers and purged many who were unwelcome in the Maoist leadership. These purges were the most violent aspect of the Cultural Revolution, but they were much less visible than the flamboyant rallies in the heyday of the Red Guards.

By May 1968, as the Red Guards were being dispatched to the countryside, the Cultural Revolution's mass mobilization of social protest came to an end. Mao signaled his shift against continued attacks on authority: "We must believe that more than 90 percent of our cadres are good or comparatively good. The majority of those who have made mistakes can be reformed."

The Communist Party's Ninth Congress, in April 1969, marked the reestablishment of a kind of political normality. The purge of conservative leaders opened the way for promotions of loyal Maoists to top Party positions. Nearly 70 percent of the surviving members of the eighth Central Committee were not included in the ninth, which was chosen by the new Party Congress. Some twenty-five of twenty-nine provincial Party first secretaries lost their jobs. Jiang Qing and the other civilians who constituted the Cultural Revolution Group enjoyed a new elevated status. So did the top leaders of the People's Liberation Army, especially in the wake of the border battle with the Soviet Union over a disputed river island in March 1969. Chief among these was the minister of defense, Lin Biao, named as vice-chairman of the Communist Party and, as Mao's "closest comrade in arms," treated as his putative successor.

The remaining years of the movement shared a common rhetoric and familiar gestures, yet were different in quality, as Maoists were concerned with consolidating their power, rather than winning it. Central-level politics were fluid. Although the Party railed against factionalism, obvious divisions split the civilian radicals, pragmatic officials under the leadership of Prime Minster Zhou Enlai, and military officers (with their own internal divisions). All competed for the attention of Chairman Mao, who was the great balancer of competing voices.

China looked more harmonious from outside than at the heart of Party headquarters at Zhongnanhai. After five years of political turbulence, the nation was shocked anew by the violent death of Lin Biao in September 1971. Lin (or more likely, his subordinates) had organized a failed coup against Mao Zedong. Many details of the official story stretch credulity, but the result was a fatal plane crash in Mongolia as Lin, his wife, and son, attempted to flee China. The political consequences were a purge of Lin Biao's top aides, a public crisis of confidence, and the rehabilitations of some officials who had been purged in the opening battles of the Cultural Revolution.

The final years of the Cultural Revolution featured factional intrigue at the center, as groups jockeyed for position in the court of an ailing Mao Zedong. In contrast, mass politics were calmer than since 1966, as ordinary people backed away from the more extravagant forms of political involvement. At the ground level, China seemed more normal; at the center, more weird.

The fall of leftist military leaders after the Lin Biao affair strengthened two groups. One was the civilian activists associated with Mao through his wife, Jiang Qing. The second consisted of more moderate career officials, led by Premier Zhou Enlai. At the tenth Communist Party Congress in 1973, forty Central Committee members were rehabilitated Cultural Revolution victims, including Deng Xiaoping, once excoriated as "the number two person in authority taking the capitalist road." Liu Shaoqi, "China's Khrushchev," had died under squalid conditions in 1969. Mao had not viewed Deng so harshly, shielding him from being expelled from the Party along with Liu. After internal exile in Guangxi province, Deng was recalled to Beijing as a vice-prime minster in 1973, working with Zhou to develop a modernization program. In 1975 Deng was reinstated to the inner circle of power, the Communist Party Political Bureau's Standing Committee, certainly with an eye to Zhou Enlai's deteriorating health and the need for a seasoned replacement.

Throughout the early 1970s, elite rivalries were played out through public political campaigns. These were often abstruse, and targeted surrogate issues that stood in for conflicts between top leaders. What did a "Campaign to Criticize Lin Biao and Confucius" really mean? Lin Biao had obviously become a villain. And progressive Chinese had been happily damning Confucius as an emblem of the old society since the May Fourth movement. But why link the two? In what coded way was it a Jiang Qing–driven push against Zhou Enlai? In the aftermath of the Lin Biao conspiracy such obscurantism did little to inspire confidence.

Set against these puzzling left-backed political campaigns was Premier Zhou Enlai's final appeal for the "Four Modernizations" of agriculture, industry, science and technology, and national defense. His rhetoric was suitably Cultural Revolutionary, but the content revealed the economic practicality of Deng Xiaoping and other rehabilitated old cadres.

Zhou Enlai saw to daily administration throughout the Cultural Revolution, and he remains a person of some controversy. Was he the great moderator, who kept Mao's enthusiasms under some control? Or was he the great opportunist, a sycophant to Mao who protected some underlings while sacrificing others when useful?

Political paranoia was high. Mao's declining health (he had Parkinson's and heart disease) disengaged the one central figure who could adjudicate among rival factions. Zhou Enlai died in January 1976; April demonstrations in his memory in Beijing's Tiananmen Square enabled radicals to persuade Mao to purge Deng Xiaoping a second time. The minister of public security, Hua Guofeng, who had risen with the Cultural Revolution, was named acting premier and first vice chairman of the Party. By June, Mao was too feeble to receive foreign visitors, and both his voice and his handwriting had become very difficult to understand. When the Tangshan earthquake killed a quarter of a million residents of that North China city in July, the superstitious began to wonder about the loss of the traditional "mandate of heaven."

At Mao's death on September 9, 1976, there was a quick showdown between rival factions. Hua Guofeng became the chairman of the Party. One group of Mao's supporters arrested another. The leading civilian radicals—Mao's widow, Jiang Qing, the literary official Yao Wenyuan, the Shanghai boss and deputy premier Zhang Chunqiao, and the Party vice-chairman Wang Hongwen—were arrested in a coup organized by the heads of the army and Mao's bodyguard. The radicals, newly designated to be the "Gang of Four," were initially accused of undermining the Cultural Revolution, but China had in fact began a long process of disavowing Mao's last great mass movement.

Interpretations

Mao expected the Cultural Revolution to last a year. Many argue
with some eloquence that the Cultural Revolution in fact ended
with the suppression of Red Guard activism in 1968. Yet Mao and
his allies continued to refer to the Cultural Revolution after the
end of mass mobilization, and the Party declared the movement
to have ended only in 1977. The end date is important. If we limit
the Cultural Revolution to 1966–68, many of the events of the
following eight years (opening to the West, education expansion,
infrastructure investment) look more like precursors of the reform
period that did not get under way officially until 1978. If we treat
the 1966–76 period as a seamless whole, then the distinction
between radical mass mobilization and the reestablishment of
Party control is obscured. This book respects the rhetorical unity
of the Cultural Revolution decade, but with the caution that in
politics, culture, economy, and foreign relations, one must discern
sharp differences between its radical opening and its longer
consolidation period.

Analysis and critique of the Cultural Revolution began long
before the movement ended. Early on, radicals who believed the
movement did not go far enough pressed for a broadening of the
attack on power-holders. When Deng Xiaoping was rehabilitated
in the early 1970s, he reviewed Cultural Revolution policies in
order to tone them down. But during Mao's lifetime, both leftist
and rightist analyses were defensively couched in the Chairman's
own language.

Three broad explanations appear for the causes of the Cultural
Revolution: (1) conflict within the political elite, (2) tensions
within Chinese society, and (3) China's international position.

Among the elite conflict approaches, Mao-centered accounts have
been popular with the public, although less with scholars. While
the Cultural Revolution was in full swing, many portrayed Mao as

a brilliant battler for the revolutionary masses. After his death, and especially beyond China, he has more often been represented as a monster hell-bent on sowing chaos for his selfish ambitions. An exiled Chinese artist captured this spirit by painting a vast canvas showing Mao being welcomed to hell by a party of dead tyrants, including Hitler, Stalin, and Qin Shihuangdi, the legendarily brutal first unifier of China.

Mao had both heroic and demonic aspects, and he must occupy an important spot in any interpretation. But some popular accounts depict Mao forcing his way on a whole society. These resemble the Hitler-centric views of the Third Reich that left little room for the German people themselves to be imperialistic and anti-Semitic. Mao-as-monster perspectives are also politically handy for current Chinese elites who avoid looking deeply into China's recent past. They comfort Western audiences, who often like to imagine the Chinese people as victims. But these approaches rest on bad scholarship, ignoring complex relationships for the sake of a simple message.

Like many top politicians in any country, Mao was not a well-adjusted and stable personality. He had to be at the center of things, and the Cultural Revolution made him politically indispensible. It would be foolish to disregard his pivotal role, or to ignore his personal qualities, such as his lack of friendships with other leaders or his serious physical impairments before his death. Yet simply proclaiming that the Cultural Revolution occurred because Mao was evil absolves us of any responsibility to consider other factors.

More nuanced elite studies move beyond Mao to include relations among China's top leaders. Some look to longtime factional alliances, such as the tensions of the 1930s–40s between Communists who worked together in the Red capital of Yan'an and those who worked underground, behind enemy lines. Some examine personal relationships, such as the pattern of interactions between the top military command and the Cultural Revolution's civilian leaders. This kind of analysis avoids reducing the Cultural Revolution to an assault by Mao against all, and admits the role of vengeance but also that of idealism, activism, and serious political and cultural debates. The rhetoric of the Cultural Revolution poses grandly existential questions. What should the revolution become? When and how does a revolution end? At a mundane level, the conflicts also drew in old rivalries among revolutionary comrades, personal grudges accumulated over the courses of long careers, and awkward memories of past mistakes.

A second type of explanation stresses broader social or cultural factors. These approaches presume that Chinese politics has much in common with politics anywhere: people become aware of grievances, look for opportunities to vent, and make new political deals, typically with the help of political intermediaries. Some analysts consider who benefited from the appeal for Cultural Revolution. For example, in mobilizing youth into the Red Guard movement, idealistic appeals rested atop an unspoken recognition that Chinese society had too many young people to satisfy everyone's career dreams. A baby boom engendered by peace and prosperity bore political ramifications. Some scholars have looked at the impact of previous policy choices, such as the Party's reliance upon political campaigns and close supervision of its imagined enemies. Others have emphasized the continuing influence of traditional autocracy, often with a Leninist twist. It is easy to see in Cultural Revolutionary ritual and behavior the impact of hierarchical Chinese tradition. Such cultural considerations importantly illuminate the manner in which events were played out but are less helpful in explaining why they happened.

A different kind of argument looks to international forces. For example, when the Cultural Revolution began, many Western analysts explained it as a response to the escalating American invasion of Vietnam, although the depth of the movement soon made this seem mistaken. Yet the broader cold war context, coupled with China's enforced international isolation, seems to have added pressure to China's political system. The split with the Soviet Union contributed to this isolation. Some have seen Mao's study of the Soviet Union's negative bureaucratic ways as a factor. However, the Soviet mirror probably reflected what Mao wanted to see, and it is hard to imagine that he launched the Cultural Revolution because of developments in a foreign county. The Cultural Revolution first intensified China's isolation, then began to erode it.

Most scholars of the Cultural Revolution would agree that no single approach is sufficient. The great political crisis of the early 1960s fed elite conflict, exacerbated social tensions, and pushed the nation apart from the rest of world society. It seems unfortunate to narrow our focus to a simple account of who did what to whom, ignoring the broader question of how China's decade of tumult might be related to its twenty-first century status in world politics.

Chapter 2
"Politics in Command"

"Politics in Command" was a popular Maoist slogan, reminding Cultural Revolutionaries that the correct political choice and the willpower to enforce it would make or break their movement. Three features in the standard kit of Chinese politics set it apart from Western practice.

First, the Communist Party ruled without serious challenge, enjoying a preeminence that muddies the tidy distinction made in the West between party and state. China lacked a head of state for part of the Cultural Revolution. It did not seem to matter. Despite Cultural Revolutionary rhetoric and state-sanctioned chaos, the Communist Party continued to expand, growing from 18 million members in 1966 to 34 million in 1976. However, fear of bourgeois influence shuttered the Party's ancillary organizations for youth and for women, and the eight so-called democratic parties with which the Communists superficially share state power were closed.

Second, the Party frequently turned to extra-bureaucratic techniques, especially mass campaigns that were organized outside the normal government departments, mobilizing officials, activists, and ordinary citizens to achieve a specific goal. These included such disparate targets as literacy for women, land reform, eradicating schistosomiasis (an infectious liver disease widespread in South China), writing poetry, or the building of backyard steel furnaces during the Great Leap Forward. Campaigns were good at harnessing resources but not very subtle at deploying them, as the military terminology might suggest. They were better suited for some tasks than others, but they purposely kept the bureaucracy on the defensive. In some respects the Cultural Revolution was itself an extended campaign, made up of smaller, more narrowly focused movements.

Third, the Party developed a system of labeling Chinese citizens according to their political status. The practice originated in the great land reform campaigns that accompanied the revolution, when the Party needed to be sure who was a landlord and who was a landless peasant, so that it could confiscate resources from one group to bestow to the other. The classifications became formal and bureaucratic, but with obviously important implications. After land reform, the class labels became frozen, and then were inherited by children. Subsequent political campaigns reinforced the labels, as the Party turned to "poor peasants" or their children for support, and looked askance at one-time landlords and their offspring. Other labels were added, based upon political status rather than former economic position. When the Cultural Revolution began, the "five black elements" consisted of landlords, rich peasants, counterrevolutionaries (who had resisted Communist rule), bad elements (who had committed crimes), and rightists (who had been victims of the 1957 campaign against critics of the Party).

The Cultural Revolution offers an encyclopedia of Chinese politics, including idealism, mob violence, conspiracy, social networks, bureaucratic routine, political prison, petitions, bribes, pork barrel, public theater, backroom deals, and military coups. These practices exaggerated and distorted the routines of ordinary politics in China. Theatricality, the Mao cult, rebellion, discipline, and factionalism are themes that illustrate the era's political complexity.

Theatricality

The Cultural Revolution's politics were self-consciously theatrical. The movement's public actors postured for dramatic effect on history's stage. As the movement gained traction, the seventy-two-year-old Mao Zedong emphasized his vitality and ties to the young through a highly publicized swim in the Yangzi River at Wuhan. Millions of young people quickly took to the water in emulation. After a series of carefully staged rallies of millions of Red Guards in Tiananmen Square, some young participants dramatically refused to wash the hands that had touched the Chairman. Mao called his supporters to action through grand gestures, such as putting on a Red Guard armband and writing his own "big character poster," in emulation of the tens of thousands of revolutionary declarations that young rebels pasted on public walls.

Later, when Mao wanted to rein in the Red Guards, he ostentatiously presented a gift of mangos to members of a workers' propaganda team, a new institution created to restore order by forcing peace upon warring student groups. The mangos, which had been given to Mao by Pakistani visitors, signaled that by 1968 the Chairman valued the reliable members of the working class more highly than the immature students. The organized ecstasy of the moment included well-publicized efforts to preserve the fruit so that it might be admired forever, much like medieval Christians venerating the bones of a saint.

Such theatricality had the practical purpose of disseminating broad political messages in a society with limited communications, and where Party-controlled mass media often seemed monotonous. Many of the best-staged events encouraged new forms of participation by the young, who had led orderly and passive political lives, channeled by the now-discredited Young Pioneers (for primary-age students) or the more exclusive Communist Youth League (for high school students). Red Guards reenacted the Red Army's 1934–35 Long March, tracing a

2. Mao Zedong wears the armband of the Red Guards to show his support for young rebels.

pilgrimage that bound them ever closer to Chairman Mao and to the memory of revolution. There were rituals of public humiliation for fallen officials, who were forced to stand for long periods, sometimes wearing tall hats and placards, enduring verbal and often physical abuse. The point was to break the power of the mighty but also to demonstrate to youthful rebels that they had been empowered.

The audience for the Cultural Revolution's dramatic gestures was not limited to young Chinese but extended to include the political elites themselves. The intensity of the performances helped convey to wavering members of the elite that they should not resist the movement. All states employ ritual, and China's political tradition is rich in the use of spectacle. Many peasant rebels against past emperors have worn opera costumes as they present themselves to supporters of their self-styled new dynasties, suggesting a porous line between staged spectacle and political action.

Yet the Cultural Revolution's theatrical side meant more than mere manipulation. The Maoist movement both reflected and spurred events that were quite dramatic by any terms—conspiracy, betrayal, rescue, and rebellion are among the great themes of any art. And many of the most engrossing episodes of the Cultural Revolution spectacle were performed with little or no direction, often contrary to the preferences of Maoist stage managers.

The Lin Biao affair, for example, was spectacular but not in ways that the Maoists desired. When Mao apparently wanted to put some limits on the military's political power, Lin, Mao's putative successor, saw his own influence sinking; either he organized an inept assassination plot and coup, or (more plausibly) his son, Lin Liguo, did so on his behalf. Lin Biao probably did not know much of what was going on and was perhaps drugged as he was put on a plane that crashed in Mongolia on September 13, 1971.

The drama lay not only in the conspiracy from Lin's camp, and in Lin's daughter revealing the plot to Premier Zhou Enlai, but also in the official handling of the incident. Mao and the Cultural Revolution group were shocked and appropriately concerned that news of the incident would break the confidence of millions of Chinese in the

Cultural Revolution. As Mao purged the top ranks of the People's Liberation Army, the level of central political disarray was revealed by the unprecedented cancellation of the October 1 (1971) National Day parade and celebration.

The spectacle became the absence of a planned spectacle, as Cultural Revolutionaries tried to concoct an explanation for how Mao's "closest comrade in arms" could betray him. Central authorities prepared documents that attempted to explain the scandal, but perhaps no more smoothly than the Warren Commission in the United States explained the assassination of John F. Kennedy. Only Political Bureau members were informed in the first week, and ordinary citizens waited for nearly a year, as the word spread throughout the nation in an elaborate and secret system of briefings. And the result was as Mao feared; enthusiastic supporters of the Cultural Revolution date their disenchantment from the Lin Biao affair. In this case, spectacle worked to depress support for the Cultural Revolution rather than arouse new enthusiasts to its cause.

At the level of elite politics, the Cultural Revolution brought personal and political ruin to three different claimants to Mao's succession. The first of these was President Liu Shaoqi, who fell from Mao's presumptive heir to a lonely 1969 death from medical neglect. Lin Biao's violent death in 1971 reminded all that China's political drama did not follow a master script, after all. The third failed successor was the civilian radical Wang Hongwen, promoted "by helicopter" at the age of thirty-eight to be vice-chairman of the Party, only to be nudged aside by the interior minister, Hua Guofeng, and later arrested as one of the "Gang of Four."

The Mao cult

As Mao Zedong's power increased, his words, actions, and image became imbued with a cultlike sanctity. Even in 1963, the army's production of the "Little Red Book" of quotations from Mao's writings presaged something unusual. Liu Shaoqi's works had also been republished for political study, but the distribution of Mao's works became an ideological tsunami. The four-volume *Complete Works* was a popular award presentation item for model workers and, as bourgeois luxuries came under question, a gift for newlyweds. Versions of Mao's writings varied by class. The government worker edition of *Selected Readings from the Works of Mao Zedong* was twice as long as the edition for workers and peasants, which had shorter articles and many more explanatory footnotes. And the Little Red Book provided pithy quotations, usefully arranged by topic to provide fodder for any political commentator, amateur or professional. Red Guards carried their Little Red Books for handy reference. Even mighty leaders waved their books at mass rallies and quoted Mao incessantly but with exemplary political nuance. The Chairman earned royalties on his works, which he apparently used as a political slush fund, self-financing some aspects of his own cult.

China's national anthem, "Song of the Volunteers," fell under a cloud along with the author of its words, Tian Han. The informal replacement was "The East Is Red," a revolutionary ode based upon a North China folk tune:

> The East is red, the sun is up.
> China has brought forth a Mao Zedong.
> He works for the happiness of the people, and
> He is the great savior to the Chinese nation.

This song had dropped from popularity after 1949. Perhaps even Mao thought that it was immodest as well as unnecessarily slighting to other Communist leaders. But it returned with a vengeance in 1966, sung at open meetings, broadcast from loudspeakers on the street, and, in 1970, beamed down to the earth from China's first satellite.

The other top Cultural Revolution song was Pottier and De Geyter's "Internationale" of 1888, the radical anthem sung by anarchists, Communists, and social democrats around the world. Qu Qiubai, head of the Communist Party in the late 1920s, translated it into Chinese. During the Cultural Revolution, no one drew attention to the contradiction between "The East Is Red" and the second verse of "The Internationale":

There has never been any saviour of the world,
Nor deities, nor emperors on which to depend.
To create Mankind's happiness
We must entirely depend on ourselves!

Organizations competed to demonstrate their loyalty to Mao. Newspapers printed the Chairman's words in red ink, and misuse of yesterday's newspaper in ways that might suggest disrespect for those sanctified words could lead to serious political criticism. Mao badges, produced by the million, were instantly collectible and tradable, as if having lots of badges might demonstrate revolutionary conviction. "Loyalty Dances" acted out one's political position. New songs included a series that set Mao's quotations to appropriate tunes. Cries of "Long Live Chairman Mao!" resounded in public spaces. Newsreels, paintings, posters, and statues fueled the cult. China was inundated with sculpture of the Chairman. Some of these works were gigantic; even though they were not very interesting as art, their huge scale was intended to awe or intimidate. Other statues were smaller, tabletop busts of China's leader. Display of his image, whether by a city or an individual, denoted loyalty and at least outward commitment to his politics.

In 1966, Mao possessed enormous moral authority with the Chinese public. People believed that his acts were motivated for the good of China, the revolution, and socialism. The Mao cult grew from this spontaneous respect, which radicals manipulated for political advantage. Mao may well have thought this public admiration was his due. Or he may merely have recognized its utility in overwhelming his opponents. He did little to discourage or disparage even the most outrageous expressions of Mao

3. Officials pledge loyalty to Mao Zedong by waving the Little Red Book of his quotations. Premier Zhou Enlai and Defense Minister Lin Biao walk slightly behind Mao. Lin further displays his fealty by wearing a Mao badge.

worship. And when the red haze of his cult was invoked for immediate political ends, his moral authority was diminished. It was one thing for an idealized Mao to fight for an idealized revolution. It was quite another for Mao to expel a fallen Liu Shaoqi from the Communist Party as a renegade.

At the conclusion of one Cultural Revolution song-and-dance show in Xi'an, the performers were presented with a plaster bust of Mao. In those years of Little Red Books and mass rallies, this gift symbolized shared revolutionary ardor. After the performers went backstage, the bust slipped from one musician's fingers and shattered on the floor. Mao's head, the most exalted fount of revolutionary wisdom, had been smashed into a pile of plaster fragments. The performers were shocked both by the sudden destruction of the Chairman's inviolable image and by the danger of serious political charges. Without a word, they gathered into a circle and ground the shards of Mao's head into dust with their feet. They understood that they had become complicit in an unspoken compact to conceal their secret deed.

One aspect of self-restraint in the Mao celebration seems odd to Westerners. Chinese carefully avoided the formulation "Maoism (Maozhuyi)." Although Maoism and Maoist seem to capture the spirit of the times, Chinese avoided them in favor of the much clumsier "Mao Zedong thought" (Mao Zedong sixiang)." Awkward in Chinese as well as English, Mao Zedong Thought represented a kind of restraint, modestly resisting the assertion that Mao had established a new "ism" on a level with Marxism or Leninism. The more awkward expression indicated that Mao had merely inherited and developed Marxism and Leninism. But one should not see too much modesty here, for Mao Zedong thought was routinely identified as a "spiritual atom bomb."

Management of the Mao cult formed its own political world. Lin Biao had based his personal political power upon manipulating Mao's image. Many of the Mao statues, for instance, bore bronze inscriptions in Lin Biao's calligraphy, praising the "great teacher, great leader, great commander, and great helmsman." Dead and disgraced, Lin was no longer allowed to share in the Chairman's radiance, and the inscriptions were stripped away. As the Cultural Revolution turned more conservative, "Mao Zedong Thought" was also adapted to less rebellious political needs. Mao's ample writings could be mined for ammunition to legitimize a ruling bureaucracy as well as to support young rebels.

The cult declined in the 1970s, along with the Maoists' effective use of spectacle. As Mao's health declined, his words became ever more oracular, mysterious rather than inspiring. A 1975 campaign focused on *Water Margin*, a five-hundred-year-old classic novel about peasant bandits. In an offhand remark, Mao Zedong said this beloved story revealed a negative example of "capitulationists." Mao's words were quoted in editorials, and the nation's intellectuals, still reeling from the early years of the Cultural Revolution, began to make tortured analyses of the novel, looking for clues as to which peasant rebel character represented which politician. Mao was not becoming senile, but he had cataracts, which made reading difficult, and made the remark to a young academic assigned to read aloud to him. The comment was noted and used, however ineptly, by Cultural Revolution radicals.

The great Tangshan earthquake of 1976 killed more than a quarter of a million people and was another kind of unplanned spectacle. It was viewed by some as an omen and by others as a disaster, which would seem to be inauspicious. Either way, the spectacle could neither be controlled or hidden by calls to "Deepen the Criticism of Deng Xiaoping In Anti-Quake and Relief Work."

Rebellion

However theatrical the gestures of China's leaders, no one should imagine that Mao snapped his fingers and called up the Cultural Revolution from thin air. The Cultural Revolution released the people's bitterness that had accumulated since 1949. Protracted tensions divided the political elite about how China should handle its revolutionary heritage and the burdens of economic development. These tensions were palpable to other citizens, if often indistinct. The social impact of political tensions was accelerated as they interacted with demographic factors. Peace and prosperity had boosted the numbers of young Chinese, and the rapid expansion of schools meant that large numbers of youth were educated and ambitious for good, non-agricultural jobs. But the 1949 revolution installed a set of relatively young leaders. Most were still in place and blocking job promotion opportunities for the younger generation. At the same time, the schools and universities were filled with frustrated and generally unhappy people, following the impact of the 1957 anti-rightist campaign that targeted teachers as "rightist elements."

Youth were thus easy for Maoists to mobilize at the outset of the Cultural Revolution. Most young urban Chinese took part. The great majority of Red Guards were high school students. Urban Chinese today of a certain age were almost certainly Red

Guards; a sixteen-year-old Red Guard would have been born in 1950. They were not organized by the state but instead sprang up spontaneously. Maoists then extended their political patronage, enabling the movement to spread even more quickly.

One of the signature tools of the Red Guards was the "big character poster," a poster-sized political essay displayed on a public wall. Big character posters could be polemics, exhortations, announcements, or revelations of past political behavior by officials under attack. Red Guards often turned to radical allies in the Party for leaked documents and information as they wrote. Mao Zedong wrote his own big character poster—"Bombard the Headquarters"—to underscore his support for the nascent Red Guard movement. Before long, the posters were supplemented by Red Guard newspapers and magazines, full of exposés, beyond the control of Party-run media still under conservative influence. The information revealed was generally accurate, with records of high-level meetings and ample quotations from speeches liberated from Party files. These items were often taken out of context or given the worst possible interpretation, but they were not simply fabricated.

Red Guard participation was a political act, but it was also a form of teen rebellion, opening possibilities for experiences that would otherwise have been forbidden. To facilitate the "exchange of revolutionary experiences," China's rail system provided free transportation to Red Guards in the autumn of 1966. "Revolutionary tourism" enabled young people to travel for the first time, visiting distant cities in the name of revolution. The initial mood was youthful exhilaration, buttressed by tough, militarized lingo as former members of the now disbanded youth league reimagined themselves as "Red flag Combat Groups" and "May 16 Revolutionary Warriors." Such grandiose names sometimes masked only small groups of friends sharing an interest in sports or radio. They strengthened their resolve with one of Mao's favorite quotations from the novel *Dream of the Red Chamber*: "He who is not afraid of death by a thousand cuts dares to unhorse the emperor."

Some of the mindless violence of the early Cultural Revolution flowed from the fact that the country had apparently been turned over to gangs of high school students, and no one dared rein them in for fear of seeming counterrevolutionary. August and September 1966 saw a Red Guard rampage, including a rough search for imagined class enemies. In Beijing, Red Guard teams raided more than 100,000 homes in search of reactionary materials, and they forced intellectuals and some who had earlier clashes with the regime to make self-criticisms. Some Red Guards beat people with belt buckles and tortured them with boiling water. In Beijing, 1,700 died. The Tianjin Party secretary, the commander of the East China Fleet, and the minister of the coal industry all died after criticism meetings. There were notorious cases of suicides after Red Guard beatings, including that of the celebrated novelist Lao She. Famous veteran officials were in high demand for ritual criticism meetings, in which the revolutionary masses would voice their hatred for purged leaders. The vice-premier Bo Yibo, head of the State Economic Commission, was dragged out for a hundred struggle sessions. His wife, unable to bear the strain, killed herself. Yet the majority of the millions of Red Guards were not violent, and many spoke out against violence, though with mixed effect.

Given the near universality of Red Guard participation, it is not surprising that they developed serious internal divisions. Everyone claimed to be a "revolutionary," including the children of officials under Maoist attack. One notorious Beijing Red Guard unit, the "United Action Headquarters," advocated a "bloodline" theory. Children of workers, poor peasants, and revolutionary cadres were said to be natural revolutionaries, while children of capitalists and landlords could never overcome the taint of their birth. The bloodline theory neatly sidestepped Mao's calls for focusing on "capitalist roaders" within the Party by deflecting attention to the already vanquished enemies of the revolution. The bloodline theory was suppressed, but the tendency to scapegoat the vulnerable remained. For some young Chinese this meant "drawing a clear line" between themselves and family members of bad class background or with complex political histories (such as a cousin in Taiwan, or service in the Guomindang army). For nearly everyone, it meant that members of the "five black categories" (landlords, rich peasants, counterrevolutionaries, bad elements, and rightists) were held at a distance, even if they were not actually abused.

The Red Guards flourished within a short time frame. "Red August" of 1966 was their heyday, when most of the violence against teachers and officials took place. The destruction of cultural property and raids on privileged households was limited to the early days of the Cultural Revolution. Horrible as the violence was, this opening rage of the Cultural Revolution burned out soon, as Maoist authorities strained to limit these public assaults. One should not imagine a decade of beatings and murders. Although most Red Guards did not beat people, those who were violent then turned their fury against rival Red Guard factions. Red Guards manufactured weapons, or seized guns from the army, including Russian weapons in transit to Vietnam. By 1968, this phase of the Cultural Revolution was over. Young urbanites were being shipped to the countryside "to learn from the poor and lower middle peasants."

Red Guards were not the only rebels. Junior officials joined the rebel ranks in large numbers, along with many who had grievances with the policies of the Seventeen Years. Activists from the ranks of temporary workers, denied the full benefits of permanent workers, used the Cultural Revolution to demand redress. They failed, but the possibility of factory-based unrest alarmed the authorities. Later, when Maoist leaders despaired of their student allies, they cultivated a set of working-class rebels who would be politically stable.

We should not simply dismiss these rebels' desire for radical democracy. They did not seek Western-style procedural democracy, with careful voting systems and protections for individual human rights. It was an anti-authoritarian movement, perhaps China's greatest experiment in participatory democracy, and aspired to a democracy of results, not procedure.

Discipline

"Politics in Command" disciplines as well inspires rebellion. Mao was surprised by extent of Red Guard violence. The Red Guards were a clumsy political tool: young, unruly, and difficult to deploy with any precision.

A superior model for seizing power appeared in January 1967, with the establishment of the "Shanghai Commune." This month-long venture to bring together Shanghai's proletarians was ostensibly inspired by the 1871 Paris Commune. It created a political base for three radical politicians: the propaganda official Zhang Chunqiao, the literary critic Yao Wenyuan, and the factory security man Wang Hongwen, all of whom were later excoriated with Jiang Qing as the Gang of Four.

Rather quickly, the Shanghai Commune model was supplanted by a second nationwide model, the "Revolutionary Committee." Revolutionary committees applied some real heft to the problem of unity; they were organized around a "triple alliance" of mass organizations, army representatives, and veteran officials loyal to the Cultural Revolution. The army was the enforcer in negotiating these deals, and worked patiently to find agreeable radical rebel groups and acceptable veteran cadres to create a new and Maoist local government. Even with army participation, this was a laborious task, as the Cultural Revolution had unleashed social forces that proved difficult to contain. These involved local rivalries, unbridled ambition, or political vanity. In one region of Tibet, an alliance was troubled by an unbalanced nun who experienced visitations from a goddess and who commanded armed followers who, in turn, chopped off the arms and legs of their factional enemies.

The army began to restore order by negotiating a local peace in each province. The army initially preferred to be neutral. Continued violence and disorder eventually drew it more deeply into local administration. One critical moment was the crisis during the summer of 1967 in Wuhan, where a near civil war had broken out. When a Beijing leader attempted to negotiate, he was kidnapped and had to be rescued by airborne troops. Other incidents of armed battles between thousands of young civilians broke down the army's reluctance. Most provinces had new Revolutionary Committees by summer 1968.

The army had entered the Cultural Revolution gingerly, by providing armed guards for nuclear and other military research facilities, and for cultural monuments under threat from Red Guard vandals. When Red Guards began arming themselves with weapons seized from trains headed to Vietnam, the army's reluctance dissipated. By summer 1968, the army's patience turned into ferocity as it crushed Red Guard groups unwilling to bow to its leadership.

The greatest violence of the Cultural Revolution came not from Red Guard brutality but from Maoist suppression of spontaneous mass organizations. In late 1967, the Cultural Revolution Group organized an investigation into a bogus "May 16 Conspiracy." This led to the arrest of leading radical politicos, charged with a plot that never took place. As the campaign spread to the provincial level, millions were investigated and tens of thousands killed. A related campaign to "purify class ranks" between 1967 and 1969 killed even more, as political and family histories were scrutinized for political sins. It was a bad time to have Overseas Chinese connections, or a sister who had married into a formerly capitalist family. This viciousness partially reflects the tenuous hold by China's newly promoted leaders coupled with their zeal in striking down potential rivals to their new positions. The new Revolutionary Committees consolidated their own power by demobilizing mass politics, beginning with organizations that resisted their legitimacy. Much violence took place in suburban or rural counties, where it was less visible than the early Red Guard violence. Hong Kong citizens, for example, noted bodies floating downstream to the mouth of the Pearl River. To many observers, however, violence against radicals may have seemed less noteworthy than violence against intellectuals and officials.

Discipline assumed less violent forms for most people. Political study became highly formalized, with everyone required to memorize texts, hold small group discussions, and compose public diaries of their ideological progress. Such practices built upon a long-standing culture of criticism and self-criticism in which people were expected to make ritual acknowledgement of their political shortcomings. This too became a performance art but had

打倒派性，斩断黑手！
无产阶级革命派联合起来！

4. As the faction-prone Red Guard movement was disbanded, this poster idealized two workers, staunchly urging unity through the study of Mao Zedong's works: "Overthrow factionalism, chop off the black hands! Unite the proletarian revolutionaries!"

Confucian antecedents in its disinterest in the inner soul and focus upon actual behavior.

Refuge in personal networks

Every Cultural Revolution faction waved the banner of Mao Zedong, giving a superficial appearance of unity despite a reality splintered into factional struggles of great uncertainty. Dangers arose as opportunists looked for the main chance, and citizens were persecuted for their politically questionable backgrounds.

With normal institutions disrupted, citizens at all levels turned increasingly to personal networks for security. Indeed, networks based upon kinship, shared native place, education, or work experience exist in all politics. These have long played an extraordinary role in China, despite state efforts to supersede them with "objective" and incorruptible criteria. The Cultural Revolution's universalistic rhetoric was undermined by its distrust of regular institutions, perhaps guaranteeing that personal connections came to dominate.

Among elite insiders, personal alliances intensified after the shocks of the Lin Biao affair and Mao's failing health. Even if personal connections (*guanxi*) are not in play, most Chinese presume they are and will explain the most mundane of local or national developments by who knows whom. For example, Jiang Qing and the Party security chief Kang Sheng came from the same county in Shandong province. Was this shared birthplace more important than any common political position? Many Chinese assume so and argue that it at least put their ideological alliance on a firmer footing.

The search for personal security was equally strong among ordinary citizens, especially in the new cynicism that followed the death of Lin Biao. Gifts and bribes rather than political zeal (or alongside the profession of political zeal) became means to secure a "back door" advantage, from better housing to specialized medical care, or for transferring a city child away from agricultural labor and back to town.

Politics turned nasty even for committed Maoists. Anxieties brought the theme of revenge close to the surface. Alexandre Dumas' 1844 revenge novel *The Count of Monte Cristo* found wide readership in an era when Western art enjoyed little favor. Indeed, the Chinese title (*The Monte Cristo Record of Gratitude and Revenge*) heightens its appeal to an audience hoping for security in a vicious and unreliable public world. The count, Edmond Dantès, makes his own justice, mocking the presumption that Western laws are morally superior to the East's web of personal relationships.

Jiang Qing may have been ambitious and difficult, but Mao relied upon her because he did not fully trust anyone beyond his personal circle. For all her faults, she was loyal. As she put it at her trial, "Everything I did, Chairman Mao told me to do. I was his dog. What he said to bite, I bit." In the 1970s, Mao also turned to a nephew, Mao Yuanxin, who became a leading official in the key industrial province of Liaoning.

At the very end of the Cultural Revolution, following repeated blows against conventional political institutions, the leaders of the post-Mao coup acted primarily because they wanted to be rid of their rivals but also from anxiety. Even though they had a majority in the Political Bureau, they feared that a majority of the Central Committee might support Jiang Qing and her allies in a showdown. And in defending their act, the conspirators posited a personal network, the "Gang of Four," which had a somewhat shaky basis in reality. It was not much of a gang, as three of the four did not even support Wang Hongwen over Hua Guofeng to be Mao's successor. But few were unhappy to see the imperious Jiang Qing removed, and the four, along with Lin Biao's generals, became the public scapegoats for the Cultural Revolution.

Chapter 3
Culture: "destroy the old, establish the new"

Why did Maoists think a Cultural Revolution in the arts was necessary? The 1949 seizure of political power and subsequent control of the economy had not truly empowered the working class. Once-stalwart veteran revolutionaries had been softened by the attractive yet corrupting culture from China's feudal past or from foreign bourgeois nations. The Maoist prescription was to limit these "sugar-coated bullets" while fostering a new and vigorous art that was truly proletarian in form and content.

On the eve of the Cultural Revolution, Mao complained that the Ministry of Culture had become the "Ministry of Dead Mummies." The dead mummies of China's heritage became a prime target of the Red Guards. They searched private homes for signs of feudal or bourgeois influence. A divide separated the early heyday of the Red Guards from the longer period of control and consolidation. Later policy limited the role of traditional or foreign art but was far less successful in replacing it with new works. Mao's wife, Jiang Qing, led the creation of revolutionary model theatrical works, which did find a popular audience through a formula of modernizing Beijing opera music, gender equality, and militarization.

Destroying the four olds

The destroyers of cultural objects were almost all Red Guards, and their frenzy of smashing took place between mid-August and the end of September 1966. Young people competed in opposing the "four olds" (old customs, culture, habits, and ideas). The four olds embraced symbols of China's traditional, premodern society, such as artworks celebrating Confucian elitism. These were roundly denounced as "feudal" at a time when the old society was still a memory for many, and its visible heritage included not only classical paintings and string-bound books but also elderly ladies with bound feet. The savagery of this aesthetic response to Mao's call for Cultural Revolution is perhaps best understood as youthful ignorance and bravado, mixed with a generalized anxiety that counterrevolutionaries wished to restore the old society.

Red Guards searched households of suspected enemies of the revolution, including more than 100,000 homes in Beijing. As word of these raids spread, many citizens preemptively destroyed some of their potentially incriminating possessions. The Red Guards did not steal because they were motivated by pure revolutionary ardor. If something was obviously valuable, the Guards turned it over to the state. But neither were they art critics, and when in doubt they often chose to tear or burn an object. Politically doubtful books were pulped. The destruction of national treasures caused by the young rebels is incalculable, but many personal items, including family genealogies, paintings, books, phonograph records, and religious images, were also lost forever.

Many Red Guards did not approve of or participate in raids on the homes of the "five black categories" (see chap. 2). Many also were repelled by violence against teachers and school officials. In many cases, the state intervened to protect major monuments. Premier Zhou Enlai stationed military guards at important cultural sites; even such leftist leaders as Chen Boda and Qi Benyu helped limit destruction. In some cases, local people intervened

Zhang Hua, "Report on Destroying Books," *Fuzhou Wanbao* (April 18, 1989)

I am a teacher you can say is addicted to books, yet I once participated in their destruction. I have no way of logically explaining this enormous mistake. The time was high summer in 1966, the place was the paper factory where I worked. I had already been swept out of the school, ordered to go through a period of labor. One day left me with a turbulent feeling. When I walked into the factory I didn't hear the usual sounds of the trucks delivering waste materials. The entire hundred-square-meter factory was filled with a great heap of books: foreign-style books bound in hard covers, old-fashioned thread-bound books, and paper-bound books. I approached the pile and looked at the volumes spread before me. I was angered that the book at the very top was the *Works of Du Shaoling*, which I had long admired. Rummaging through the pile, I found the *Book of Odes*, *Shaoming Wenxuan*, *New Poems from the Jade Terrace*, and *Su Dongpo Yuefu*.

The foreman called a meeting before we began work. He read some quotations from Chairman Mao and made our job assignments. "The authorities said that these are four olds; the whole lot is feudal, capitalist, or revisionist. They were sent here after searches of homes and are to be pulped. . . . Those we don't finish will be left for the next shift."

For a moment I had no reaction, then Master Shao nudged me: "Go to vat number one and tear up those thick books." I hesitated, then walked over to the mouth of vat number one and squatted down, seeing only such big books as *English-Chinese Dictionary*, *Russian-Chinese Dictionary*, *Advanced Mathematics*, and other foreign-language books whose names I do not recall. I leafed through several pages, unconsciously stopping. I lifted my head and saw Master Ding and Master Jiang deftly tearing apart books, cutting the bindings with small knives, and scattering the pages into the mouth of the vat, just as naturally as if the truck had delivered a load of waste paper. Seeing me dawdling, they called out sharply: "What do you think you are doing? Get to it!" Both hands trembling, I tore pages out of books, but I felt a stab of pain, as if I were tearing at my own heart. I gave some thought to hiding that *Works of Du Shaoling*, but feared that Red Guards might unexpectedly attack, and I didn't want any trouble. Before long, I was listlessly ripping apart books, putting the torn pages into the mouth of the vat. With my own eyes I witnessed nearly two tons of books turned to yellow pulp, stirred back and forth in the process of making pulp.

From the beginning of the destruction of the four olds, I heard that our factory alone had nearly twenty carts of books for the boiler. No matter whether red or white, all were swallowed up by the boiler!

Chinese and foreign history have sufficient precedents for destroying books, but Qin Shihuangdi did not burn works on agriculture and medicine, and Hitler only burned books with "anti-German ideology" and books on sex (Lu Xun, "A Comparison of Chinese and German Book Burning"): both were selective burnings. The pattern and spirit of these burnings was clearly different from our destruction of books—except for a batch of red books, all could be included in the category of the four olds and consigned to destruction. Moreover, our formula for destroying books—meticulously using them as waste material—is vastly superior to Qin Shihuangdi and Hitler. Who can say that they were more savage than we?

to protect historical treasures, such as the Confucian family sites in Qufu, Shandong province. Students and faculty hid the Central Conservatory's library of recordings. Many families found ingenious ways to conceal prized items.

Caught up in the same net with the four olds were emblems of bourgeois art, including imported books and music as well as modern Chinese products of the 1911–49 period. Works associated with the Soviet bloc were castigated as revisionist. Nationalist in tone from the outset, the Cultural Revolution's mass mobilization phase played up a nativist strand never far from the surface in Chinese society. Red Guards in the northeastern city of Harbin doggedly pulled down an entire wooden Orthodox church, a relic of Russian influence.

Red Guards harassed their fellow citizens who had hairstyles that were not conventionally plain and thus presumed to be "bourgeois," sometimes providing an unwanted trim on the street. They rejected pointed shoes, tight pants, perfume, pets, gambling, jewelry, dirty jokes, and gambling games. Sturdy People's Liberation Army greatcoats replaced Hong Kong tailoring to set the new style in fashion. Red Guards changed street names, leaving the Soviet Embassy on Anti-Revisionist Road and renaming the street of the Foreign Ministry as Anti-Imperialist Road. Premier Zhou Enlai had to draw upon his full diplomatic skills in order to prevent red traffic lights from becoming a revolutionary signal to "go" instead of stop. Individuals also changed their names, ridding them of feudal odor. Babies were given names redolent of martial and revolutionary virtue, "Red Hero" instead of "Precious Jade."

The destruction of the four olds, although brief, was tied to some of the most notorious violence. Red Guards have subsequently been blamed not only for their own misdeeds but also for earlier acts of vandalism against China's past, including the Guomindang activists of the 1920s and the Western art plunderers of the imperialist era. The well-known Beijing ruin of the Emperor's Garden of Perfect Brightness (*Yangming Yuan*), burned by a British-French army in 1860, for example, is sometimes wrongly blamed by foreign tourists on Red Guard destruction.

Parallel to the drive against the four olds was a burst of revolutionary art-making, especially by Red Guard students from conservatories and fine arts academies. Enthusiasm was more important than quality, although often the best student calligraphers were drafted to write big character posters, the better to attract readers.

As central authorities worried about how to keep the Red Guards within bounds, they tried to limit spontaneous street performances, which succeeded only in whipping up crowds. By December 4, 1966, Zhou Enlai met with rebels from several arts organizations, claiming that Mao Zedong had told him that street propaganda is not easy to do well and could even be unsafe in Beijing's large crowds. Zhou Enlai assured the Red Guards that it would be better for everyone for the city to organize the big propaganda performances. By February 1967, central authorities sought to tighten control by declaring that young artists "must altogether cease going outside to exchange experiences." Artists were to return at once to their original schools and workplaces to prepare revolutionary art for workers, peasants, and soldiers.

Mao and other leaders of the Cultural Revolution were not pleased by the national furor over the four olds and the household raids, because these directed attention away from their main target, "representatives of the bourgeoisie" in positions of power. In fact, members of China's political elite had cultural tastes that would have disappointed many Red Guards. Mao loved traditional opera and old novels, enjoyed some standing as a calligrapher, and exchanged poems with other old revolutionaries. One of his rivals, the economics official Chen Yun, was a major patron of the ballad singing of the lower Yangzi region, *pingtan*. Kang Sheng, charged with Party security work, was an outstanding painter of chrysanthemums.

Mao wanted a more serious redirection of Chinese culture than railing against wearing pointed shoes and playing violins. He complained in 1963 that revolutionary China's arts accomplishments were too few, despite considerable effort: "Isn't it absurd that many Communists are enthusiastic about promoting feudal and capitalist art, but not socialist art?"

Jiang Qing and the model theatrical works

Mao put the promotion of socialist art in the hands of his wife, the former actress Jiang Qing, who organized a series of model theatrical works. Jiang Qing is best seen as a kind of producer, working with a group of experienced singers, dancers, and composers, including the minister of culture Yu Huiyong. These works joined a long-standing trend of modernizing the arts by selectively incorporating Western elements, such as orchestras and ballet, here in the service of revolution instead of entertainment. Jiang Qing was proud of her new productions but intolerant of competition. Although she began her work prior to the Cultural Revolution, it did not become dominant until the purge of the civilian left and the end of mass mobilization. Jiang Qing presented a set of eight model works to the nation in May 1967, as the Cultural Revolution was forcibly demobilizing its Red Guards.

There had been other dramas, some performed as street theater but also others with grander ambitions, such as a musical play in Wuhan called *Bombard Wang Kuang, a Power Holder Taking the Capitalist Road*. A more notorious work was *Madman of the Modern Age*, a play staged in Tianjin. Its subject was Chen Lining, who had been put in a mental hospital before the Cultural Revolution for keeping critical notebooks on the writings of Liu Shaoqi. When Liu fell from power, Chen was freed and celebrated as a liberated political prisoner. Wang Li and Qi Benyu of the Cultural Revolution Group backed the play. But Chen Lining also kept notes critical of Mao, which were discovered just as the purge against the Cultural Revolutionary Left was gaining momentum. Jiang Qing declared that Chen Lining was no hero, not even a

madman, but a counterrevolutionary. The play became tainted
with alleged associations to the May 16 conspiracy, an anti-Maoist
cabal that did not exist but was invented to topple rising leftist
politicians such as Qi and Wang.

Jiang Qing was jealous of any competition to her meticulously
planned arts project and extremely touchy about spontaneous
Red Guard creations. She took advantage of the end of the Red
Guard movement to halt its most extreme cultural nativism. Thus
Jiang Qing intervened to protect two imported art forms, which
Red Guards attacked as bourgeois: oil painting and piano music.
Jiang Qing saw both as opening possibilities for transforming
Chinese art. Although she was happy to see individual artists'
and aficionados' art suffer, she was not willing to allow
unsophisticated Red Guards deprive her of the deep and brilliant
colors of oil painting or of the rich sound palette of Western
music. Twin 1968 campaigns hailed an oil painting of *Chairman
Mao at Anyuan* and the piano version of the model opera *The
Red Lantern* as new revolutionary achievements. Each featured
a new young artist. The painter Liu Junhua had represented a
saintly looking young Mao on his way to a 1924 miners strike;
nine hundred million copies of this painting were plastered
all over the nation. The pianist Yin Chengzong, a prizewinner
in Moscow's Tchaikovsky competition, created a piano
accompaniment for one of Jiang Qing's most popular model
works. Actual imported Western painting and music remained
controversial throughout the Cultural Revolution. However, no
one would question adapting their basic methods and materials,
now purified for the revolution.

The Red Lantern was one of the initial set of eight "model
theatrical works." Five were Beijing operas on revolutionary
themes, modernized not only in story but also in orchestration and
presentation. Two were ballets and one was a symphonic suite,
both newly imported forms to China, although Jiang Qing played
down their foreign links.

These model theatrical works were extremely popular and were performed all over the nation. The ballet *The White-Haired Girl*, for example, tells of a young peasant, driven to hide in the mountains by a vengeful landlord until her hair turns white. Villagers mistake her for a ghost. But she returns home only after the revolution destroys the landlord. The theme is revolutionary but also feminist (although the Cultural Revolution did not employ this term). Although the music is clearly Chinese, it is scored for the instruments of a Western symphony orchestra.

In contrast to traditional Chinese opera, the music became louder, departing from the small ensembles of traditional string instruments. But a greater contrast was the content of the new works. While traditional opera emphasized moralizing stories from the legends of ancient dynasties, the new theatrical works were set in the present, drawing lessons from the revolutionary era.

The radicals chose the performing arts for their innovations because literature, the art that has historically been closest to power in China, was more firmly controlled by their adversaries. Seizing power in the theater was not only easier but Jiang Qing's own background as an actress gave her a self-confidence about the stage that she lacked for other arts. Chinese opera is also a more broadly popular genre than literature, making it more suitable for populist reforms. Finally, the operas lent themselves to model presentation, including amateur and film versions, in a way that novels or poems did not. These choices gave the arts of the Cultural Revolution immediate vitality and political direction.

Others of Jiang's aesthetic choices were highly personal. She disliked folk songs and passed up an opportunity to incorporate tunes of proven popularity into her productions. She also systematically auditioned the instruments of the symphony, deciding that the tuba was ugly and thus found no place in her program. The composite art she produced mixed kitsch and sophistication, and it fit the May Fourth tradition of modernizing China through its culture.

Cultural Revolution aesthetics

More significant than Jiang Qing's personal quirks, the Cultural Revolution tapped into some long-standing traditions even as it called for a radical new art. The principle of art for art's sake has never reigned supreme in China. Westerners often believe that art should be spiritually uplifting, that reading Tolstoy's *War and Peace* or gazing at the Venus de Milo helps create a more cultivated and sensitive person. This hope is humanistic: that the arts enable us to understand fundamental truths about the human condition. The West also has a lesser tradition of art intended to persuade, such as Francisco Goya's horrific drawings of the Napoleonic wars or Sergei Eisenstein's films about the Russian Revolution. In China, message art is a major tradition. Chinese artists of all political persuasions take it for granted that their art should comment upon public life, either as paid propaganda workers or as dissident critics of the regime. Art need not have political content, but most artists would agree that art should edify and educate. Indeed, some regard it as a political act when artists turn inside to personal, meditative themes.

The Cultural Revolution's assault on commerce fit comfortably with the notion that business tainted art. In fact, much of China's premodern arts world was associated with commerce. But commercial activities were often disguised as gifts or unrecorded, so that all could maintain the genteel fiction that art was above money. The Cultural Revolution encouraged a cult of the amateur, disdaining the elitism of professional artists. Radicals imagined that workers, peasants, and soldiers could become artists and performers whose participation would enact a new revolutionary culture. In reality, Jiang Qing's insistence on high standards led to the unpublicized use of professionals as tutors for the amateur artists, carefully hidden from public view.

The amateur ideal of Maoist activism did not envision art to be a recreational pleasure. Art was much too earnest for such a revisionist attitude. Art was fiercely utilitarian, with little room for any dreamy quality, a striking absence in a movement with such utopian ambitions. But if art was not for pleasure, pleasure nonetheless emerged, especially in the culturally impoverished countryside. People enjoyed watching and performing the operas. Many enjoyed the unambiguous clarity of the message. Indeed, the absence of artistic alternatives may have heightened the intensity of the experience. Others, however, were continually troubled by the constricted boundaries of acceptable art. Why was it anti-revolutionary to enjoy a painting of a goldfish?

The Cultural Revolution had little tolerance for Chinese aesthetics that played with decoration, complexity, and the display of an easy virtuosity. Cultural Revolution art was too puritanical to convey much sense of play. One sees this especially in traditional handicrafts. Already threatened by the revolution, which eliminated the wealthy collectors who bought lacquer ware, cloisonné, or ivory or jade carvings, the Cultural Revolution forced an end to products bearing such names as *Guifei the Drunken Concubine*, *The General and the Minister Make Peace*, *The Eight Immortals* [of Taoism], or *Big-Bellied Buddha*. The renowned Jingdezhen porcelain factory learned to produce the (highly coveted) Mao badges. A Beijing factory came up with new designs for revolutionary statuettes, including popular characters from the model operas, the model soldier Lei Feng, and the Canadian martyr to China's Revolution, Norman Bethune. Yet virtuosity persisted, now turned to the revolution. One of Hong Kong's mainland-owned department stores displayed an elephant tusk, carved with incredible delicacy and precision into a massive battle from the Long March. Tiny Red Army soldiers charged the enemy, tossing hand grenades all the way to the point of the tusk. But the market for such revolutionary luxury goods was small.

5. *The Rent Collection Courtyard* was a collection of one hundred clay statues, depicting a rapacious landlord, his agents, and suffering peasants in Sichuan province.

The Cultural Revolution did little to undermine China's ancient ideal that good rulers are concerned with culture, which provided legitimacy to Maoist efforts to redefine China's arts. Yet it created some dissonances. Given the aesthetic inclinations of many Communist leaders, the Cultural Revolution's rigid aesthetic constraints invited hypocrisy. When traditional operas were banned, Mao Zedong watched a set of specially filmed performances in his private residence. Lower-level Party leaders could watch foreign movies barred to public view, rationalized as "study." Zhu De, the politically inactive one-time commander of the Red Army, passed the Cultural Revolution watching movies by Abbott and Costello, those well-known American comedians of the 1940s. More sinister was the connoisseur Kang Sheng, a leading Mao ally who selected thousands of paintings, seal-carvings, and books for his personal collection from Red Guard raids on bourgeois owners.

Maoist art broke sharply with the tradition of looking to an idealized past. China's ideal of an ancient golden age contrasts to the Western ideal of progress, that the best is yet to come. Here the Maoists joined the May Fourth tradition of abhorring the heavy weight of China's tradition, which was seen as a vessel for feudal values. The Cultural Revolutionaries continued language reform, the drive to standardize and simplify written Chinese characters in order to reduce barriers to literacy.

Maoists broke the long reign of literature as the preeminent art form by raising the prestige of performing arts, which were less heavily weighted by the literati tradition. New stars included the singer Qian Haoliang and the dancer Liu Qingtang (later made deputy ministers of culture), and the pianist Yin Chengzong (composer of the popular *Yellow River Concerto* and deputy head of the Central Philharmonic). The celebrated novelist of the period was Hao Ran, whose *The Golden Road* sold 4 million copies in 1972, the first year it was published. But Hao is distinguished by his lack of literary companions. He was the only writer to receive royalties in early 1970s, enjoying a lonely material treatment equal to that of ministerial level officials.

Finally, Cultural Revolutionary arts are remarkable for rejecting traditional sexism. Many works prominently feature a strong female protagonist, underscoring the movement's push to include women in leadership positions. Perhaps inevitably, some saw fawning portraits of Jiang Qing in the fighters of *The Red Detachment of Women*, or *The Red Lantern*'s resourceful and courageous heroine, Li Tiemei.

Political control and the fear of spontaneity

The arts reforms were also a system of political control. This does not refer to the control over individuals, who seem to have been quite capable of sorting out when they were merely singing along

with Mao or just having a good time. Instead, it refers to the arts'
role in reinforcing a sense of shared national participation.

The Cultural Revolution was a period of radical decentralization.
This was partially deliberate. The economic policies of self-reliance
made a virtue of the need to avoid overloading China's fragile
transport system. Decentralization was also inadvertent, as in the
near collapse of the national administrative structure when the Party
establishment came under fire. In contrast to centrifugal political
and economic trends, Jiang Qing's arts were highly centralizing.

The Chinese name for "model theatrical works," *yangban xi*,
borrows farming terminology for trial agricultural fields to suggest
a role for experimental theater. Like an outstanding strand of rice,
the model works were to be copied and spread throughout the
nation, with little room for local variation. Beijing published books
that carefully specified the costume design, the measurements of
props, and the stage movements for each production. The operas
were disseminated much like the huge identical statues of Mao,
always with the same arm lifted, as if directing traffic. Eventually
regional adaptations of the Beijing operas appeared, but strikingly
few variations appeared even when Jiang Qing's favored genre
of Beijing opera was rendered into Cantonese or other regional
opera. Although most Chinese learned the official Beijing-based
Mandarin dialect in school, local dialects of Chinese remained in
wide daily use, and were closely tied to beloved local art forms,
such as regional opera. The model works were spread through
the nation via many media, including film versions. Millions of
rusticated city youth amused themselves and their peasant hosts
by singing arias from the operas.

Especially before the death of Lin Biao in 1971, the
militarization of Chinese culture contributed to the sense
of an art in service to the entire nation. The army took over
the Ministry of Culture in 1965, in the run-up to the Cultural
Revolution. Later on, whole cultural ensembles, including

祖 国 的 好 山 河 寸 土 不 让

6. "We will not give up a single inch of our beautiful fatherland."
People's Liberation Army musicians perform patriotic songs in the
open fields.

the Central Philharmonic Orchestra, performed in military
uniforms as they sought army patronage and protection. The
army's own highly professional performing arts ensembles also
performed the new works.

Maoist central control over culture enabled the center to
portray a nation of greater unity than was in fact warranted.
The Cultural Revolution superficially homogenized ethnic,
economic, and even gender differences. China's enormous
population and vast area underlie great regional cultural
specialties. These often divide broadly between north and
south but with provincial or even county-level arts specialties
in opera, storytelling, painting, and crafts. Some local cultural
preferences were discouraged, if not suppressed prior to the
Cultural Revolution. The noisy, insistent culture flowing from
Beijing distracted attention from the many local variations that
reemerged in practice, as a result of administrative chaos and
economic decentralization.

Jiang Qing's cultural reform prized central control over spontaneity. She and her co-workers sought to create an art that appeared inspirational without actually remobilizing mass politics. One of the consequences of this impossible task was a lack of artistic diversity, a shortage of new art works in the eyes of even dedicated Maoists. Jiang Qing's production team, headed by the new minister of culture Yu Huiyong, could not raise output rapidly enough to keep Chairman Mao from sniping at them.

It is often said that Cultural Revolutionary arts consisted only of Jiang Qing's eight model stage works. This is an exaggeration, but it points to cultural shortage. More revolutionary operas appeared, plus a piano concerto, a symphony, three sets of sculptures, a couple of ballets, and some spoken plays and films, as well as around one hundred novels, local ballads, and puppet theater. There were propaganda posters, paintings, and songs. In addition, other arts included Mao's poetry, the classic novel *Water Margin*, and ancient legalist literature reprinted during the campaign against Lin Biao and Confucius. For the politically privileged, foreign movies and novels were available. Yet it is bizarre to be able to jot down most of the art available to the citizens of such a populous and cultivated nation over a whole decade.

Several factors slowed creation down, including the enormity and grandiosity of Jiang Qing's goal. Her imperious and vindictive personality reminded all that art is easier to control than to produce.

The Cultural Revolutionaries sincerely wanted a thriving, enthusiastic, and radical culture to supplant all that had gone before. But they feared what mass participation might unleash. In 1971 Zhang Chunqiao urged a modest loosening of arts supervision, instructing that new songs need not be approved by central authorities. But in 1976, the Ministry of Culture still had an office for evaluating new songs, including six hundred tunes attacking Deng Xiaoping (freshly purged from his post as vice-premier) and "right deviationism."

Penalties for artists were levied only after an essay or painting had crossed "a line." But the lines were rarely marked clearly, making artists all the more anxious. Bosses remained cautious, not only because of *their* bosses but also because Maoism operated informally, by encouraging outraged citizens to complain vigorously about ideological transgressions. The system worked effectively when there were millions of ardent Maoists; when political enthusiasm waned after the Cultural Revolution, so did the effectiveness of the censorship.

Having few outlets for publication made it easier to police the work of writers. By 1973 there were only fifty magazines and newspapers, down from 1,330 in 1960. The collapse of establishment organizations in 1966 brought down the media that they sponsored. But breaking the professional associations of artists and other intellectuals meant that the Cultural Revolutionaries worked without the support system that had grown up during the Seventeen Years. Many intellectuals assisted the new regime. But dispirited artists were not compelled to write, paint, or choreograph.

Other new initiatives, such as peasant painting, began only late in the Cultural Revolution. Such ventures developed slowly, in part because of the awkward need to use formally trained (but ideologically discredited) professionals to train new peasant artists.

Some of the doctrines governing work on the model theatrical works formed obstacles. It was tricky to depict the enemy, for fear of making landlords, Japanese invaders, and "hidden class enemies" of the present day look too interesting. A "theory of three prominences" set rules for artists: "Among all the characters, give prominence to the positive characters; among the positive characters, give prominence to the main heroic characters; among the heroes, give prominence to the central character." In practice, this meant that heroes monopolized the action, flooded with light from the sun, as in so many posters of Mao Zedong.

Artistic spontaneity reappeared during the April 5, 1976, demonstrations mourning the death of Premier Zhou Enlai. Many people posted poems among the wreaths placed in his honor in Tiananmen Square. More than a few poems fiercely opposed Jiang Qing and her allies. Even these initially spontaneous poems, finally published after Mao's death as a part of an organized campaign against the Cultural Revolution, reminded readers how profoundly art had become enmeshed in politics.

The perils of cultural work

Older artists and their children often became targets of the Cultural Revolution. Many came from highly educated families who had initially supported the Communist Party in 1949. But the double blows of the 1957 Anti-Rightist Campaign and the Cultural Revolution made it difficult for the Party to attract enthusiasm and utilize their knowledge.

The dangers of working in the arts rose through the Cultural Revolution. By 1969 the Party was defensively criticizing the false "theory that cultural work is dangerous." This was the belief that the bourgeoisie regarded culture as its hereditary domain, intimidating workers and revolutionary intellectuals. The Party argued that the struggle in culture was especially complicated, which was not a reassuring message to nervous artists.

How much trouble could cultural work be? For example, Chen Minyuan was a twenty-four-year-old researcher at the Acoustics Institute of the Academy of Sciences. As a child, he met Guo Moruo, the left-wing dramatist and archaeologist who taught young Chen how to write poetry. Later, Chen sent poems to his mentor, and these seem to have ended up mixed in files with poems from another of Guo Moruo's correspondents, Mao Zedong. In October 1966, Red Guards produced a mimeographed edition of *Unpublished Poems of Chairman Mao*. Of twenty-four poems, Mao had actually written two; ten were Chen's. When

Chen heard Red Guards reading his own poems outside the Academy of Sciences, he spoke up, only to be labeled a "practicing counterrevolutionary" for daring to claim the Chairman's work as his own. Chen was imprisoned until the fall of Lin Biao, when he was allowed to return to the Academy. Even then he was not allowed to resume scientific work until 1978. No one dared to ask Mao if he had written the poems.

Many abandoned art to escape from politics altogether. Two of China's great writers, Qian Zhongshu and Shen Congwen, put down their pens in 1949. Few were able publicly to refuse artistic commissions outright during the Cultural Revolution, but many found it practical to be slow and uninspired. Most artists were state employees, and even malingering artists continued to draw state salaries from their work units. The violinist Zhang Xianghe avoided entanglement. With only music in his background, he had no political pigtail to grab. A physician provided him with a certificate of long-term illness. He had four hospitalizations and spent a lot of time teaching violin to his two children.

Many bookish Red Guards found refuge in the arts after being sent to the countryside. In many villages, illiterate peasants had great respect for education and chose to give young intellectuals space to practice their calligraphy or to read classic books, which enjoyed a brisk underground exchange.

Still other Red Guards used the arts as a welcome road out of the countryside, or at least out of daily work in the fields. The push to expand touring song and dance troupes created new demand for musically talented young people. A similar trend took place in urban factories, where worker musicians and painters were released from regular duties for rehearsals and performances to stimulate their workmates to greater efforts. These trends led to a sharp rise in the price for used violins and accordions.

At Mao's death in 1976, Jiang Qing and her allies perched on a very narrow political base. Powerful as culture can be, its strength plays out only over the long term; it rarely trumps steel mills or soldiers in a showdown. Deng Xiaoping assembled reports from unhappy artists, then used these to try to undermine Mao's support for Jiang Qing.

The challenges that Maoist arts posed to Chinese culture were enormous. But these arts issues were more nuanced than a simple question of destruction versus preservation. Nor did the divisions reduce themselves to the Communist Party versus the artists. Both fell together, and both returned together. The Cultural Revolution was both destructive and reconstitutive. Its end did not assure an era of artistic freedom.

Looking back, the Cultural Revolution built upon a powerful, existing May Fourth program of radical modernization, with its rejection of weighty burden of "feudal" values. Yet the Cultural Revolution also forsook the complete Westernization advocated by the more extreme May Fourth activists. Instead, the Maoists cultivated a Chinese nationalism buttressed by Western techniques.

Looking forward, the Cultural Revolution created a rather homogenized cultural audience, honed by didactic messages and shaped to exclude niches that appealed chiefly to region, class, or ethnicity. This would later become a commercialized mass market for entertainment, continuing the quest for technical innovation under the banner of modernization. More importantly, the Cultural Revolution was one blow toward breaking the privileged role of the intelligentsia in political life. The relentless hammer of marketization further undercut their standing. Even the Cultural Revolutionary stress upon the performing arts now appears as part of a longer-term, global trend by which the role of the humanist intellectual has been diminished, first by political direction, then by market indifference.

Chapter 4
An economy of "self-reliance"

"Self-reliance" was the slogan that guided China's Cultural Revolution economy, reflecting both China's isolation as a nation and Maoist desires to substitute abundant human labor for scarce capital as a strategy for economic development. China's economy fared better than post-Mao reformers admitted, but it did not conform to typical developmental patterns; Chinese had low incomes but much higher literacy and life expectancy than such poverty usually suggests. China's self-reliance joined an ideological Puritanism to restrict individual consumption for the sake of public investment. The Cultural Revolution initially disrupted the economy. But order returned to China's cities after 1968, sending millions of Red Guards to work in the countryside, still home to 80 percent of the population. Although the economy grew significantly, the gap between city and countryside remained problematic. The Cultural Revolution was a last hurrah for distinctively Maoist economic initiatives. Yet Maoist investment in infrastructure and human capital provided an indispensible base for China's subsequent economic opening to the outside world.

Poverty and economic growth

China was poor; the per capita income in 1978 was $859 in 2010 dollars. Yet it was relatively egalitarian. The revolution had diminished differences in wealth by eliminating the classes that lived most extravagantly. Rural landlords had been dispossessed through land reform. The extended lineage organizations that sustained their power were vastly weakened. Private capitalists lost control over their assets in a 1956 nationalization of property, although the state continued to pay off bonds issued in exchange.

The Cultural Revolution intensified the egalitarianism. Red Guards attacks on "bourgeois" life styles merely underscored existing state policies. Repeated restrictions upon small business created a profound shortage of consumer goods for everyone. In 1952 China had one restaurant for every 676 people; by 1978 there was only one for every 8,189. Ration coupons were needed to buy cotton cloth, grain, meat, fish, cooking oil, and eggs, frustrating some but discouraging hoarding and ensuring more equal access to scarce items. Bureaucratic rank replaced wealth in aiding access to goods and services. But except for the luxuries enjoyed by the very top leaders, the range of official privileges was restricted.

Manual work was celebrated in a land where gentlemen traditionally made a display of the exemption from physical labor by wearing long fingernails and long gowns. Maoists sought to soften China's poverty through campaigns to "remember past bitterness," in which older workers and peasants would meet to tell young audiences how they had suffered before 1949.

Should socialism be a framework for egalitarianism in consumption or should it be an engine for increasing production? It is difficult to be both at the same time. Socialist governments have labored to resolve or at least obscure this tension. Maoists, recognizing that China could still achieve only egalitarian poverty, elevated individual austerity and Spartan consumption into an ideal to free funds for greater public investment. The Cultural Revolutionaries often allocated these investments inefficiently; they presided over a planning regime that dismissed service sector needs, tolerated large regional gaps, and allowed only a slow rise in living standards.

Even so, the economy during the Cultural Revolution was not the disaster that is often described. China's gross domestic product (GDP) grew nearly 6 percent annually, a slightly slower rate than during the earlier years of the People's Republic but still a respectable performance. The figures appear low only by comparison to the post–Cultural Revolution boom economy. It is difficult to construe these figures as a catastrophe.

China's Cultural Revolution growth rate stands up to comparison during the same period with two other poor Asian giants, India and Indonesia. All three nations faced similar problems and constraints in industrializing large agrarian societies. China grew somewhat less rapidly than Indonesia but about twice as fast as India. All three grew more slowly than Taiwan, South Korea, Singapore, and Hong Kong. These four smaller regions later became known as Asia's "tigers" for their rapid growth (8–9 percent), following a formula that mixed foreign aid and investment with the export of consumer goods to wealthier nations. These small and briskly authoritarian states, with access to sea transport, integrated with ease into the growing international market for textiles, chemicals, and electronics for Western consumers.

The disorder of the Cultural Revolution's first two years halted growth and even shrank the economy. As early as September 1966, top leaders tried to prevent rebel disruptions to the economy by demanding that everyone should "grasp revolution,

Chinese Economic Growth (GDP) Before, During, and After the Cultural Revolution

1952–1965	6.85%
1966–1976	5.94%
1977–2009	9.63%

Economic Growth Rates (GDP) for Three Asian Giants, 1966–76

China	5.94%
India	2.95%
Indonesia	6.95%

promote production." The dispersal of the Red Guards by 1968 was accompanied by the slogan "the working class must exercise leadership in everything," when the restoration of Party authority led to two years of extraordinary growth. The remainder of the Cultural Revolution brought moderate, if uneven, increases, save for 1976, when political disruptions again contributed to a production decline.

The dichotomy of utopianism versus pragmatism may not be as absolute as some might have it. For all its egalitarian appearance, Cultural Revolutionary China retained a doggedly developmentalist agenda. Mao shared this agenda with his rival Liu Shaoqi and the policies of the Seventeen Years (see chap. 1). Similar developmentalism would be continued through Deng Xiaoping's reform program. Despite differences in approach and emphasis, China's leaders agreed that the state's job was to make China rich and strong as quickly as possible.

Economic ideals and rhetoric

The Cultural Revolution was more a political than an economic movement. Maoist radicals established firm control over the mass media, cultural, and propaganda sector but had less control over ministries that oversaw production. Radicals dominated the voice of the Cultural Revolution, without always controlling the levers of production. As a consequence, there is an economic rhetoric that speaks for the ideals of the Cultural Revolution but does not

Annual Economic Growth (% of GDP) during the Cultural Revolution

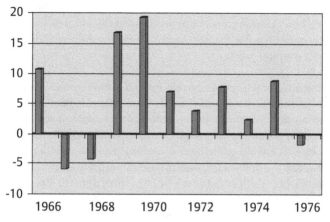

necessarily capture its economic realities. Radicals shouted loudly for China to move leftward. By and large it did, yet factories continued to manufacture products in familiar ways, and central planners continued to allocate resources, although with greater sensitivity to the ideals of the movement. Deng Xiaoping, excoriated early in the Cultural Revolution as "the number two person in authority taking the capitalist road," was rehabilitated in 1973 and took charge of the government from 1974 until his second purge in 1976. The late Mao period was more practical than its rhetoric suggests.

"Self-reliance" (*zili gengsheng*, or "regeneration through one's own efforts"), like much of the Maoist program, bore the heritage of Yan'an, the wartime Communist revolutionary capital in the poor and remote northwest. That birthright stressed intense campaigns to cope with the extreme isolation and limited resources. It also embedded the Communist Party into local peasant culture. Reviving this ideal during the 1960s summoned up memories of the revolution, but now it was applied to the national scale and greater sophistication of the People's Republic.

The Maoist era of "self-reliance" also adapted to the sudden cut-off of foreign aid. When the dispute with the Soviet Union heated up in 1960, Moscow suddenly recalled 6,000 advisors, halting work on 156 large economic projects. Soviet advisors took the blueprints home with them. And so self-reliance became China's only practical course.

Promoters of self-reliance were suspicious of extreme divisions of labor. Instead, Maoists advocated "all-round development" within economic units. Provinces were supposed to become self-sufficient as a way of minimizing transport costs and bottlenecks. For the nation as a whole, self-reliance demanded import substitution, learning to manufacture goods in China, from train locomotives to antibiotics, which would otherwise be purchased abroad. Boosting domestic production cut waste of scarce hard currency and stimulated local innovation. Import substitution was popular in Asia and Latin America in the 1960s, before the rise of neoliberal free trade approaches. And so while China's advocacy was unyielding, the policy itself was unremarkable for its era.

Maoists swaddled their economic pronouncements in revolutionary rhetoric by implying that the only alternative was capitalism. But the clash of Mao and Liu Shaoqi was no showdown between socialism and capitalism, however much recent commentators may want that to be. Maoists and their adversaries agreed that the state should hold a commanding role over the economy, albeit with important nuances in emphasis.

How did China differ from the command economy of the Soviet Union? China was much more decentralized (partly due to poor transport), with significantly smaller-scale firms. Decentralization pursued national and regional autonomy far beyond the Soviet system. China offered a narrower range of material incentives and emphasized personal austerity, slowing growth in personal consumption. Finally, China championed the development of native technologies alongside advanced technology, which it called "walking on two legs," such as efforts to mix Western-style medicine with traditional Chinese herbs and acupuncture.

Maoists distrusted material incentives, although they were not so successful at limiting them. Peasants divided their communal harvest earnings according to a work-point system, which assessed farming skill, diligence, and political commitment. Urban workers, on the other hand, continued to be paid by the existing work-grade system. The method for ranking and paying officials remained.

Meanwhile, Cultural Revolution rhetoric embraced a heaven-storming, militant style, in which sheer revolutionary willpower would triumph over material constraints. In Marxist theory, this is known as "voluntarism," which speeds up the forces of history with a well-placed shove. Song and dance troupes entertained workers and boosted morale. If revolutionary songs inspired them to work harder, so much the better. Jiang Qing herself was the patron of a Tianjin village, Xiaojinzhuang, which stressed popular participation in the arts to stimulate greater production. Deng Xiaoping mocked the Xiaojinzhuang amateur visions of transforming the world: "You can hop and jump, but can you jump across the Yangzi?"

Xiaojinzhuang was a model unit, massively publicized to teach the country a particular lesson. Models were carefully scouted, polished, subsidized, and protected. The two most celebrated models were a village in Shanxi province and an oil field in Heilongjiang province: "In agriculture, learn from Dazhai, in industry learn from Daqing."

The Dazhai production brigade became a model for expanding agricultural production through its painstaking creation of terraces on its steep hillsides. The Party used political campaigns to organize production calendars. Abandoning cash incentives in favor of moral persuasion, the Dazhai model substituted labor power and political will for the capital that China lacked. Dazhai developed into a revolutionary tourist site, where visitors came to learn. It was not always clear how a well-watered, flat village on the Lower Yangzi plains might improve its farming, beyond emulating its political spirit. Dazhai's leader, Chen Yonggui, rode the celebrity of his village to became a vice-premier. Although he was never a political heavyweight, Chen's promotion symbolized Maoist desires to raise peasant status.

The Daqing oil field in Liaoning became its industrial counterpart as a pacesetter in production. Forceful leaders such as "Iron Man" Wang Jingxi were described as heroes for their legendary hard work in a punishing environment. At Daqing, workers drilled for oil in the bitter cold of Manchurian winters. They famously mended their coats in testimony to Maoist austerity and to discourage waste elsewhere. Yet despite the publicized

7. Peasants of the model Dazhai Production Brigade take a break from field work for a round of collective political study, reading Mao's words together. Leader Chen Yonggui wears a Mao badge.

similarities to Dazhai, the petroleum industry was among China's most capital-intensive and poorly suited to emulation. But Daqing produced half of China's petroleum and played a major role in the economy, even if its production collapsed after the Cultural Revolution. These models recalled the Great Leap Forward of the late 1950s (labor plus political will can overcome all restraints) but within much more modest limits, and without the sense that a new world was just over the horizon.

An equally celebrated model was not a place, but a person—the soldier Lei Feng. An orphan of parents victimized by the Japanese and landlords, he found a home in the Party, where he became a paragon for good deeds, such as darning the socks of his military comrades while they slept. He died (if he really existed) before the Cultural Revolution began, but his diligent study of Chairman Mao's works, frugality, and selfless dedication to the revolution made him a popular model. Lei Feng was an everyday hero and became a kind of patron saint of idealized civility.

If models were vehicles for the ideals of the Cultural Revolution, the basic elements of social control for urban citizens were their work units, the offices and factories that employed them. Workplaces provided not only secure jobs but also subsidized housing, health care, pensions, schools, vacations, entertainment, bus tickets, and other services. Unsurprisingly, this vast range of vital services encouraged dependency and placed bosses in the position to assign favorable housing or even to participate in marriage arrangements. A system of residence permits, initially introduced to keep track of population movement, turned into a control device for preventing peasants from flooding the cities after the 1959 famine. Urban residence permits became highly cherished, especially when millions of young city dwellers were being sent to the countryside. Adroit and lucky workers often managed to hand down urban jobs to their children. Peasants, however, were members of agricultural production teams and brigades, which were collectively owned (in contrast to state or private property). Thus peasants were not employees and had fewer perks than the highly subsidized urban workers. In addition, peasants were often harder to discipline.

A chronic urban-rural gap

Maoism's egalitarian thrust could not eliminate China's persistent material inequalities. Some were regional, with concentrations of industry in the northeast and in coastal provinces. Self-reliance demanded that each community make the most of its own resources. Areas with more resources do better under such a regime, so it is not surprising that mountainous peasant villages remained poor, or that remote areas populated by ethnic minorities had a hard time improving their status.

Another persistent inequality was the "great wall" that separated peasants from urban workers. An urban household registration was required to obtain a city-based job. Four-fifths of the population was rural; farmers were effectively stuck in the countryside. The Cultural Revolution drove even more people from the cities to the countryside. In fact, many of the former Red Guards ended up returning to the cities within two to ten years. Urban bureaucrats were sent down to work in "May 7 Cadre Schools," but they actually continued to earn their urban salaries while they forged new agricultural projects in isolation from local peasants.

Rural life between 1962 and 1981 was organized by groups of around thirty households, which made up a village or neighborhood. These production brigades used work-point systems to divide their harvest incomes (one harvest per year in North China; up to three in South China). Production brigades belonged to larger communes of around two thousand households, which provided administration and social services. This system was not necessarily the most efficient at growing crops, but it was good at mobilizing agricultural inputs (labor, fertilizer, water) and organizing non-agricultural activities, such as credit, education, health care, and rural industry.

The villages, for all their diversity, reenacted a revival of class struggle, in which the classes were essentially historical, rather than ongoing. Members of local poor and lower-middle peasants associations provided the basis for local Communist Party power. This majority scrutinized a small minority who belonged to the five black categories. Few villages had any rightists, but if so they were intellectuals. But all villages had family members of former landlords and rich peasants, few of whom constituted any threat to the revolution. Most were victimized until after the end of the Cultural Revolution in both significant and petty ways. A landlord's daughter could not join the Party or militia and would be unlikely to find recommendations for educational opportunities. A rich peasant's son would find few brides willing to assume the stigma of his class. Before 1949, the poorest male peasants could not marry, so many peasants probably regarded the new order as rough justice. Sometimes the class language of the Cultural Revolution simply masked persistent older forms of village politics, such as lineage rivalries. In broad terms, the rural class relations had mutated into something akin to a caste system, where barriers to social relations and intermarriage became deeper than actual property distinctions.

Seventeen million youth went down to the countryside, some as volunteers prior to 1966, but most as demobilized Red Guards who had little choice. They were ostensibly to learn from the "poor and lower-middle peasants," that is, those who had benefited from the Communist land reform. The down-to-the-villages program helped to tone down Red Guard arrogance, while addressing a problem of urban unemployment. There was inevitable resentment against the program, but it was muted in public, mostly limited to grumbling by young people and their peasant hosts. Yet when Lin Biao's son justified the assassination plot against Mao, one of his complaints dealt with sending youth to the countryside, a practice that, he asserted, was really a form of disguised unemployment.

Some villages welcomed the educated new arrivals and treated them with respect. Others regarded them as nuisances, unskilled farm hands, extra mouths to feed who contributed little labor. Many urbanites schemed immediately about ways to escape. Some formed lifelong bonds with villagers that have lasted to the present. Some even married locals, committing themselves to remain for life. Most were shocked to discover how very poor the farmers were. When the former Red Guards saw how little their hosts had to eat and wear, they realized that city life was more prosperous than they had known. Indeed, the ratio between urban and rural incomes was around three to one.

Even Maoists could not make peasant status desirable. Young Chinese competed hard for worker and soldier jobs. Either of these offered protection against farm labor and defined a new upward mobility. Universities were closed in the radical opening phase of the Cultural Revolution. When they resumed accepting new students after 1970, applicants were selected not by national entrance examinations but by workplace recommendation and family background. When present-day journalists report that intellectuals or officials had to work in a factory during the Cultural Revolution, they typically miss the key point that factory jobs were generally seen as a movement upward, rather than down. China has a long tradition of idealizing rural life as pure and idyllic, yet holding actual peasants in disdain. The Cultural Revolution era was more pro-peasant than most, but it could not avoid this urban snobbery, despite the vast debt the Communist Party owed to peasant revolutionaries.

The Cultural Revolution continued state exploitation of agriculture in order to finance industrialization. The state set prices for compulsory grain procurement quotas, but farmers had to buy manufactured goods at relatively high prices. Farming thus did not pay, but restrictions on geographical mobility tied farmers to the land. As industry grew more rapidly than agriculture, pressure for greater food production increased. Agricultural productivity constantly constrained Cultural Revolution policymakers, who sought to increase efficiency through terracing new fields, harnessing new labor power, and amplifying ideological encouragement.

Between 1966 and 1976 irrigated fields increased by nearly one-third. Not all of them were efficient, for the Dazhai model was sometimes applied thoughtlessly to the wrong kinds of terrain. But it did enable crop increases by leveling land, which facilitated irrigation and which would have been impossible without Cultural Revolution mobilization of peasants to dig ditches during what had formerly been the winter slack season. Fertilizer use increased greatly, though it was of relatively poor quality and nothing like what was to come in the reform period. Important innovations in seed varieties paralleled "green revolution" developments elsewhere in Asia.

Improving the workforce

The greatest economic success lay in improving China's human capital. Maoists substituted abundant labor for scarce capital whenever possible; they extended this approach by improving worker health and education, and by drawing more women into the workplace.

Public health achievements were notable. Life expectancy at birth, a mere thirty-five in 1949, increased to sixty-five by 1980. This was a dozen years longer than in India and Indonesia. Most of the increase came from improved nutrition, lower infant mortality, and control of infectious disease. Nearly two million peasants trained as "barefoot doctors" in an ambitious rural paramedic network. These barefoot doctors were not especially well-equipped or sophisticated, but they were accessible and their services nearly free, as they worked alongside fellow villagers. They were the most celebrated part of a vast increase in rural medical care over the preceding period. By the end of the

8. Children line up for smallpox inoculation from a barefoot doctor. China expanded public health in the countryside during the Cultural Revolution.

Cultural Revolution, two-thirds of China's hospital beds were found in the countryside.

Leaders pressed to integrate Western-style medicine with traditional and less expensive practices such as herbal medicine and acupuncture. Earlier efforts to integrate Western and Chinese healing had never gotten very far because of resistance from medical professionals, who regarded herbal medicine as peasant ignorance. The Cultural Revolution broke the capacity of the experts to resist the "Reds" in medicine and in other technical fields. Scientists were asked to test and refine the best indigenous practices. Acupuncture entered the hospitals, while low-cost manufactured drugs entered the tool kits of the barefoot doctors. The result was roughly analogous to Cultural Revolutionary arts programs, which addressed Chinese themes through techniques found in Western oil painting and symphonic music. In medicine, however, the hybrid reflected both Chinese modernism and nationalism, along with a search for programs that would be both effective and low cost.

Similar achievements in education had a massive impact. Chinese adult literacy (those fifteen years and older) was 43 percent in 1964 but rose to 65 percent in 1982. This may understate the achievement; 90 percent of Chinese ages fifteen to nineteen were literate in 1982. This compares to 56 percent of same cohort in India in 1981, with an adult literacy rate of 41 percent. China's rapid rise in literacy reflected an unprecedented fifteenfold increase in rural junior middle schools between 1965 and 1976 (becoming literate in Chinese requires an additional two years of early education beyond norms for alphabetic languages).

As with the health system reforms, the overthrown school experts would not have approved the new education program. Schools blended education with work, in an effort to make the classrooms relevant to students' lives. Work-study programs were antithetical to such Confucian traditions of education as the memorization and commentary on classic texts, and to the idea that education's goal is to produce a sophisticated elite. The new system also discouraged child labor by using work points to divide the collective harvest, reducing an incentive to keep children from school in order to boost family income.

This positive view of Cultural Revolution education goes against the conventional wisdom, which typically rails against the Maoist closure of schools, although primary schools had remained open. In fact, high schools resumed by 1967, as Maoists were desperate for ways to get the Red Guards off the streets. The schools that were closed were the universities, which stopped admitting new students until 1970. Thus the Cultural Revolution massively expanded the lower school levels for people at the bottom, but severely constricted universities. The university hiatus could be regarded as a temporary suspension of the cultural capital that had advantaged elite families.

An economy of "self-reliance"

77

From 1972 to 1976, universities enrolled new students not on the basis of a national examination but by the recommendation of local officials based on the applicant's family background and workplace performance. Local examinations often helped sort out the applications. This cohort of "worker-peasant-soldier" students was disparaged after 1978, but it represented a serious effort to get China's universities up and running once more.

Political resistance to reopening the universities was fierce. In 1973 Zhang Tiesheng, a former high school student looking for a way out of the countryside after five years of unwanted peasant work, applied to attend university in Liaoning province. During an examination in which he was doing poorly, Zhang notoriously abandoned the official questions and turned in an essay denouncing "bookworms" who did nothing useful while he had labored in the fields. His antic resembles desperate students around the world (if you cannot answer the question, write something else). But in the late Cultural Revolution, Zhang became a leftist hero for daring to swim against the elitist tide, and he enjoyed a brief but stellar political career.

Increasing access to basic health and education improved the quality of the workforce; expanding women's paid employment increased its size. The Cultural Revolution insisted that "women hold up half the sky," as it pushed back against traditional sexist barriers to employment. In the cities, nearly all young women joined the workforce. Family incomes rose in a period when individual wages were stagnant, reconciling male family members to greater female empowerment.

Working women also shifted the urban birth rate into decline, following a peak in the 1960s. Mao's enthusiasm for an ever-greater labor supply initially discouraged population control. But this caution ended by 1971, when a new population policy began, cutting fertility rates in half by 1978. The rustification of the

深夜不眠

9. "Still awake deep in the night." The certificates on the wall denote a peasant leader, and the sleeping child reveals a mother who studies late in the night to acquire technical knowledge.

Red Guards aided the decline by removing a fertile cohort from its normal social setting. The state also demanded that people have later marriages, fewer children, and longer gaps between births. Such measures forced couples to plan their children but were far gentler than the better-known one-child family policy, which did not begin until 1980. Deng Xiaoping's post–Cultural Revolution reforms abolished rural China's collective farming, education, health, and social systems, including the "five guarantees" of food, clothing, fuel, education, and a funeral. Thrown on their own, rural families began once more to regard their children as a kind of old age security system. In response, the state initiated ever harsher measures to restrict population growth.

Women bore the burden of these post–Cultural Revolution policies and were also first to lose their jobs through the closure of state industries. Both of these "reforms" were accompanied by attacks on Jiang Qing, which were intensely misogynous as Cultural Revolution advances for women were put in retreat.

Cultural Revolution expansion of health care, increase in primary education, and drawing women into the workplace all strengthened the quality of China's workforce. Resulting increased productivity would benefit any economic strategy, including the export-driven reform program of Deng Xiaoping. The educated elite, often lacking sympathy for the common people and unhappy at the erosion of its own privileges, passively resisted these egalitarian changes during the Cultural Revolution and fiercely criticized them afterward.

Industrial investment

Self-reliance encouraged regional autonomy, in part to cut transport costs. Nonetheless significant improvements strengthened the transportation infrastructure. In 1968 the Yangzi River Bridge opened at Nanjing. Completing this unfinished Soviet-aid project made it possible for the first time for rail traffic to cross China's great river in East China, thus ending the need to move trains onto ferries. Beijing's first subway line was completed in 1969. Thousands of new bridges and roads improved rural movement of materials and goods.

Rural industry became a dynamic part of the industrial sector, with new commune-based enterprises producing goods such as chemical fertilizer, farm implements, irrigation equipment, cement, electric motors, and hydroelectric power. These received significant state investment and tax exemptions. The township and village enterprises critical to post–Cultural Revolution reforms grew out of these rural industries.

Self-reliance has its green aspects. Poverty discourages waste, and consumption of local goods cuts transport pollution. But the Cultural Revolution's relentless developmental agenda was hard on the environment, as self-reliance also pushed every community to grow grain, even where this was environmentally unsound. "Grain as the key link" was bad for grasslands, and the aquifers of the North China plain were seriously stressed. Lakes shrank as farmland was extended. Against this trend, forestation increased biomass in the 1970s. And the level of environmental damage, harmful as it was, worsened quickly after the Cultural Revolution, as Chinese developmentalism shifted to a market paradigm of rapid growth.

Given Maoist resistance to consumer goods, industrial development stressed heavy over light industry, such as clothing. Growth was respectable, but investments were often inefficient. The so-called "Third Front," a secret, military-led industrialization program to build new factories deep in China's interior, was a prime example (the First and Second Fronts were coastal and central lines of military defense). Many factories were built in caves or hidden among the mountains of the southwest.

This hidden economic base against American or Soviet attack required huge amounts of capital, which might have been better spent in other regions, where construction was cheaper and local skills more abundant. But coastal investment was vulnerable to possible American bombing or attacks from the Guomindang in Taiwan. Maoists also wanted to reward still-poor old revolutionary base areas for their past services and to spread industrial skills more evenly across the nation. Lesser, but still significant, Third Front factories were built nearer the coast, in the underdeveloped mountains of Zhejiang and Fujian provinces. These also produced armaments, steel, and chemicals.

This defensive, sometimes paranoid aspect pervaded Cultural Revolution economic policy. Self-reliance was inspired by realistic anxiety of foreign invasion. At one point, the Party enjoined citizens to "dig tunnels deep, store grain everywhere." The idea was to withstand Soviet attacks on China's transport system. Inadvertent unearthing of previously unknown archaeological artifacts was the immediate result. Lin Biao's demise and the decline of military power dampened support for the isolationist Third Front. China's reconciliation with the United States eventually finished it off.

In 1971, the year Lin Biao died, China's total foreign trade reached a low point of 5 percent of GDP, but foreign trade tripled by 1975. With the end of the Third Front, Zhou Enlai and Deng Xiaoping, with the backing of Mao Zedong, initiated a great shift in economic policy, marked by a decision to import eleven large-scale fertilizer plants from the West. Zhou Enlai's speech announcing the "Four Modernizations" was a late Cultural Revolution venture. The economic transition from Mao to Deng actually began during the Cultural Revolution, not after, and it was more also gradual than the total rejection of Maoism that we normally hear about.

Without Maoist development, there would have been no Deng "miracle." The Cultural Revolution foundations for Deng Xiaoping's economic reforms included high literacy and good health, high-yield varieties of rice, and irrigation and transit projects built by all that Maoist labor. Industrial infrastructure may often have been created inefficiently, but it provided a heritage for subsequent growth. Deng inherited an economy free of debt to foreign countries. Maoist decentralization, plus the heavy blows of the Cultural Revolution against the bureaucracy, minimized the sort of economic entrenchment that blocked reforms in the Soviet Union.

Of course the post–Cultural Revolutionary reformers dealt with many inflexibilities as they privatized state firms, improved the supply of consumer goods, developed an aggressive foreign trade system, expanded the credit system, and moved beyond central planning. Maoist approaches reached a point of diminishing returns, in addition to their heavy political costs.

Asking whether the reforms really began in 1971 instead of 1978 is not a silly question. Deng Xiaoping insisted on the 1978 date, as he needed to make all of the Cultural Revolution decade look bad (including those policies that he implemented) in order to justify some of the nastiness that accompanied the turn to market reforms. Moreover, beyond China, neoliberalism has enjoyed a generation of ceaseless propaganda telling us that the market is the only way to organize human affairs. This obscures seeing that the trajectory of "post-Mao" reforms began in the middle of the Cultural Revolution.

Chapter 5

"We have friends all over the world": the Cultural Revolution's global context

The Cultural Revolution captured attention around the world, both from conservative leaders who dreaded that China might upturn the international order, and from radicals who admired China's bold experimentation and defiance of the superpowers. China claimed to have "friends all over the world," even as its isolation reflected cold war militancy. China broke that isolation through a cautious but decisive reconciliation with United States. This renewed participation in the international system set the path for economic reforms. As in so many realms, the label "Cultural Revolution" obscures very different attitudes; its international affairs included policies both rejecting and accommodating the international order.

A rhetoric of world revolution

The Cultural Revolution decade coincided with a global movement of radical politics. For Americans, black power, feminism, the hippies, and opposition to the Vietnam War defined the era. For Europeans, the Paris riots and Prague Spring of 1968 marked a broad cultural and political shift. The United States and the Soviet Union struggled to contain disruptions to their own spheres of power, and sought opportunities to make mischief within the realms of their rivals. This added an important global dimension to the 1968 Soviet invasion of Czechoslovakia, the Chile coup of 1974, wars of resistance in Africa, and the American wars in Indo-China.

China symbolized resistance to imperialism, and the Cultural Revolution seemed a bold experiment in social engineering. Mao enthusiasts in the West regarded China as opening an alternative road to either Western capitalism or Soviet top-down planning. Western protestors admired Red Guard energy; feminists borrowed the Maoist slogan "women hold up half the sky." Such perspectives may now seem romantic, but a popular Western hunger for new political models and China's isolation gave them real appeal. The issues of the Cultural Revolution seemed rather grand from outside of China: class struggle, the meaning of socialism, the future of revolutionary movements. But inside China, the practical questions on the ground resembled politics everywhere: built-up grievances, opportunities to vent, and to make new political deals.

Access to China was difficult. The McCarthy purges of the 1950s had forced the most open-minded China experts from the U.S. State Department and quieted critics of U.S. policies in the universities. The United States banned use of American passports for travel to "Red" China. The future scholars David and Nancy Milton managed to slip in via a trip to a circus in Cambodia. The journalist Jonathan Mirsky jumped from a ship at the mouth of the Yangzi River in 1969 but still failed to enter. A generation of American China scholars could approach no closer than Taiwan or Hong Kong. Europeans could travel to China, but Chinese suspicion of foreigners limited contact.

The Cultural Revolution revived Western interest in China with the allure of forbidden fruit. Maoist ideals popped up in unexpected settings, such as a senior American professor who demanded that a campus speaker show his hands to prove he had done manual labor, asking critically, "Where are your calluses?"

Although it sounded inane at the time, the query seems even odder today, as the "normal" political world has moved far to the Right. Many Westerners hoped for world revolution with China as a linchpin. Others viewed China more simply, as a moral force in a world torn by inequalities.

China's internationalist rhetoric was strong. Most Chinese studied Mao's essay "Remember Norman Bethune," in which he lauded the Canadian surgeon who died in 1939 while treating Red Army soldiers, encouraging Party members to respect foreign contributions to world revolution. China welcomed the Paris uprising of 1968, although was puzzled by its countercultural aspect. Beijing was clearly more comfortable celebrating the 1971 centenary of the Paris Commune, a more conventional worker upheaval.

China aligned itself with popular struggles in Asia, Africa, and Latin America. Black liberation politics in the United States produced great enthusiasm. After the assassination of Martin Luther King Jr., Mao issued a fiery proclamation against American racism. China also provided sanctuary to Robert F. Williams, a black separatist leader hounded into exile by the United States for seeking to turn five states of the former Confederacy into a "Republic of New Africa."

China's media insisted that revolutionary people throughout the world studied the *Quotations from Chairman Mao*. The Black Panthers purchased copies of Mao's Little Red Book for twenty cents, reselling them for a dollar on the Berkeley campus of the University of California, and purchasing shotguns with the profits. The Panthers began actually reading what Mao had to say only a few months later.

Was China a center of world revolution? Rhetorically, beyond doubt. Enthusiastic official discourse about imperialism's total collapse and socialism's approaching worldwide victory disrupted normal diplomatic exchange. Foreign diplomats in China were often ill-treated, most notoriously when a mob burned down the office of the British chargé d'affaires in Beijing. Premier Zhou Enlai raged at those who failed to control the demonstrators. China, unable to maintain the fiction of normal diplomatic relations, recalled all its ambassadors except the ambassador to Egypt.

Maoists thought seriously about China's relations to the world. Mao noted that Lenin had been mistaken to say that "the more backward the country, the more difficult the transition from capitalism to socialism." Mao believed that the West was so rich and that capitalists had ruled so long that working people labored under a profoundly disabling bourgeois influence. In a kind of weakest-link theory, socialist revolution turns out to occur in lands where Marx did not anticipate it. It falls to the Third World, with its massive population, to achieve world revolution.

Lin Biao, in a well-publicized 1965 speech, spoke of replicating China's revolution on a world scale by "surrounding the cities from the countryside." Just as the Red Army had moved from its rural bases to encircle China's major urban centers, so would the rise of proletarian nations cut off the power of the capitalist ones. A kind of globalism of world revolution emerged in Beijing decades before the counterglobalism of world capitalism.

China's critique of Soviet revisionism was deadly serious. Liu Shaoqi's epithet as "China's Khrushchev" mocked him for allegedly shying away from revolution. The nuclear test-ban treaty became a symbol of Soviet compromises with imperialism, enhancing the revolutionary and nationalist symbolism of China's own 1964 bomb.

China pretended that Comrade E. F. Hill, chairman of the Australian Communist Party (Marxist-Leninist) was a leading world statesman, dispatching no less than Kang Sheng, a leading member of the governing Cultural Revolution Group, to greet him at the Beijing airport. In fact, Hill did not even lead the real Australian Communists but rather a splinter faction encouraged by Beijing. Around the world, Communist Parties split, with Maoist factions calling themselves "Marxist-Leninist" to distinguish themselves from the "revisionists" who remained loyal to Moscow.

Cold war realities

Mao dismissed imperialism as a "paper tiger," one which only looks dangerous. But he treated it with caution. Under the radical rhetoric, China's behavior was a defensive reaction to the cold war. China did aid Vietnam, arm the odd rebel group, and cheer those who tweaked the United States and the Soviet Union. China backed underdogs in world affairs, with mostly symbolic results. Yet Cultural Revolution foreign policy was cautious and nonexpansionist. The Maoist strategy of "people's war" was profoundly defensive, stressing popular resistance to invasion, and the army was poorly suited to wield force abroad.

The United States perhaps offended China most grievously by backing the deposed "Republic of China" regime of the Guomindang in Taiwan. From his Taiwan exile, Chiang Kai-shek maintained a fictional government of mainland China, complete with such offices as a "Mongolian Affairs Bureau." American diplomatic pressure kept this rump state in the United Nations until 1971, squatting in the Security Council in place of the People's Republic.

The U.S. military presence on Taiwan was not just an annoyance but an armed threat. The United States based its troops and missiles in Taiwan, and provided equipment and training to its military government. The Taiwan government constantly crowed that it was "Free China" in order to appeal to anti-Communist Americans. The Taiwan situation replicated the U.S. relationship with other right-wing Asian dictatorships. But it was only Taiwan that launched military raids on the Chinese mainland. In 1970, Taiwan movie theaters sold peanuts in bags saying "reconquer the mainland."

The cold war had a significant impact upon China's economy. For example, Fujian province, a coastal region with long experience in foreign trade, was a poor place for Beijing to invest while Chiang Kai-shek's frogmen were attacking coastal towns. The once-major port city of Xiamen (Amoy) was blocked from development by Guomindang military bases on the nearby island of Jinmen (Quemoy). Military crises failed to alter the Jinmen situation in the 1950s. Throughout the Cultural Revolution, Communist and Guomindang armies shelled one another on a bizarre schedule of one hour on alternate days, just enough to keep the aging civil war alive. Cold war pressure made the inefficient Third Front industrialization program seem practical, at least from a strategic point of view. Reluctant to invest in cities that might be bombed, China turned its gaze turned inward.

The United States imposed an embargo on Chinese imports. Even Chinese books and magazines were difficult to obtain. Many research libraries still have Chinese publications of the period stamped with U.S. government warnings that the contents contained Communist propaganda. The Cultural Revolution also broke the traditionally profitable connection to Overseas Chinese communities, whose relatives in China were often accused of capitalism and espionage. Upgrading Chinese industry became difficult without access to foreign technology, thus strengthening Maoist insistence on discovering new applications for native ways. With limited trade, Chinese technicians attempted difficult projects of reverse engineering, in which an imported item would be taken apart to unlock its secrets. One extreme example was the deconstruction of a single Boeing 707 jet, a Pakastani plane that crashed in Western China in 1971. But China still lacked the technical capacity to match the American product.

China's pride and stubbornness created setbacks, making it more than a simple victim of the more powerful United States. When China feuded with the Soviet Union, it found itself in the unenviable position of arousing the simultaneous fury of both superpowers, far from an ideal diplomatic outcome.

China experienced the United States fighting wars near its borders in Vietnam and Korea. The United States based its troops and supported right-wing client governments in Taiwan, Japan, Thailand, and the Philippines. China had no military bases or clients in Canada, Mexico, or Cuba. China's truculent but nonexpansionist policies faced a relentless anti-Communism.

Inevitable friction between revolutionary rhetoric and cautious practice appeared in Portuguese Macau and British Hong Kong, the twinned colonies at the mouth of Guangdong province's Pearl River. Against some expectations, China had seized neither of these imperialist holdovers in 1949. China was embarrassed when Indian troops marched into the comparable Portuguese-ruled enclave of Goa in 1961, but China tolerated the colonies as part of its practical diplomacy. Sleepy Macau, with its casinos, was less of a consideration than bigger and busier Hong Kong. British law, the business talent of Shanghai refugees, and the steady flow of Cantonese labor combined to create a prosperous, intensely export-oriented economy. Hong Kong was important to China as a point of contact with the West, a link to the Overseas Chinese communities of Southeast Asia, and a conduit for foreign trade. Both colonies were home to large numbers of refugees from the Communist revolution, including supporters of the Guomindang. But they also contained well-institutionalized leftist communities, centered around schools, unions, and department stores.

Tensions within China spilled into these colonies, whose foreign rulers were challenged by popular riots, strikes, and bombs. As in the mainland, order returned with the suppression of the Cultural

Revolution's opening burst of radicalism. Portugal overthrew its fascist dictatorship in 1974 and quickly abandoned its colonial holdings in Africa and Timor. But China apparently declined to accept the return of Macau, fearing this might force Beijing to take over Hong Kong suddenly, before the Communists were prepared to absorb a large, capitalist economy. Macau remained under Portuguese administration until 1999, two years after the restoration of Hong Kong to China.

China explored strategic options to escape isolation. One was to split America's allies. France under de Gaulle pleased China by standing up to the United States, withdrawing from the North Atlantic Treaty Organization and developing an independent nuclear policy. China dreamed of openings that would allow Japan a similar autonomy, but these hopes were dashed by the U.S.-Japan Mutual Security Treaty of 1960.

China's second option was to gather support from other Third World nations. The most lasting bond was with Pakistan, which looked to China as a counterweight against India. But China's bad relations with India after the 1962 border war showed the difficulty of Third World solidarity. China worked hard to win friends in Africa, providing aid to build the Tanzam railway between Zambia and Tanzania in order to avoid dependence upon racist South Africa. Algeria proved a steady diplomatic friend in North Africa.

China had pinned great hopes on Indonesia. Under the left-leaning Sukarno government, China and Indonesia cooperated to build a Third World international presence, including a counter-Olympics called Ganefo (the "Games of the New Emerging Forces"). On the eve of the Cultural Revolution, a coup in Jakarta was followed by a massacre of Indonesian leftists, including large numbers of Overseas Chinese. Perhaps a million people were killed, with quiet American support, ending the prospect of a Sino-Indonesian alliance.

China's nuclear weapons program was designed to provide some protection when diplomatic efforts failed to reduce pressure from the two superpowers. China looked to the world much like Pyongyang or Tehran does today: isolated, surrounded, and building bombs in the face of the criticism from existing nuclear powers. Western media portrayed China as mad and unpredictable, but China's nuclear weapons fit comfortably into a foreign policy of *realpolitik*. Proposals for a joint American-Soviet preemptive bombing of China's nuclear facilities increased anxiety. Chinese leaders remembered Hiroshima and repeated U.S. nuclear threats from the Korean war on.

China's efforts to break free of encirclement had failed decisively by 1969 and the end of the Cultural Revolution's radical phase. American military aircraft flew across China (especially Hainan Island) with impunity on their way to bomb Vietnam, despite China's downing of several spy planes. The Central Intelligence Agency paid the Dalai Lama an annual retainer in order to assure continued pressure on China from Tibetan exiles, although U.S. arms drops to rebels in Tibet apparently ended in 1965. Memories of the recent invasion of Czechoslovakia remained fresh when Chinese and Soviet troops fought at the Ussuri River border in March 1969. This battle further raised the prestige of Lin Biao and the military, but pushed Mao toward reconsidering China's defiant, yet isolated, global position. By 1970 Beijing counted only a few friendly governments beyond Vietnam, North Korea, Pakistan, Algeria, and Albania. China banked on the love of the "peoples" of the world rather than their governments, but peoples do not control armies or trade.

Mao tilts toward the United States

Mao imagined a bolder step, a rapprochement with the United States that would further divide the two superpowers. The United States faced defeat in Vietnam; China offered reconciliation in order better to confront the Soviet Union. China sent a signal by inviting the American journalist Edgar Snow to stand beside Mao at the October 1 national day parade in 1970. Snow had written the best-selling *Red Star over China* in 1937, a book that introduced the Chinese Communist movement to the world. Red-baited and driven into exile in Switzerland in the 1950s, Snow welcomed the visit as vindication. Little did he realize that Mao believed he was a CIA agent. Other "people-to-people" diplomacy, such the visit of an American ping-pong team, preceded Henry Kissinger's secret trip as National Security Advisor in July 1971. Kissinger, who pretended to be ill and in Pakistan, negotiated Richard Nixon's visit to Beijing for February 1972.

Beijing won China's seat in the United Nations, enhancing Mao's strategic realignment. Third World nations had led annual campaigns in the General Assembly to expel Chiang Kai-shek's representatives. These actions had embarrassed the United States, but they failed to win enough votes until October 1971.

The new U.S.-China relationship could not be achieved without some roughness. Life-long anti-imperialists and anti-Communists had to be persuaded to put aside ideological convictions for strategic gains. Only a zealous anti-Communist like Nixon could have engineered the rapprochement with political safety; a similar observation applies to Mao, the world's most prominent anti-imperialist.

Lin Biao was unsupportive, but any resistance from the military ended with Lin's violent death. American opposition also came from those forces invested in the cold war status quo. James Jesus Angleton, the CIA's longtime head of counterintelligence, insisted that the decade-old Sino-Soviet split was a fake, a trick designed by Moscow to get the West to let down its guard.

China's deal with the United States was ambiguous in detail, yet helpful to both sides. The United States and China moved back from their allies in the Vietnam War and combined to oppose the Soviet Union. The United States agreed to remove troops and diplomatic recognition from Taiwan. China probably believed that political unification with Taiwan would soon follow, but remained disappointed. Yet removal of U.S. military bases from Taiwan enabled China to redirect investment toward coastal regions and wind down the costly Third Front program. In an unexpected outcome, the end of U.S. military backing for the Guomindang martial law government opened the way for Taiwan's democratization, moving the island even further from unification.

China continued to attack imperialism but linked it to a denunciation of "hegemony," code for the Soviet Union. Mao improvised a clumsy redefinition of the "three worlds" of global politics. The United States and the Soviet Union composed the first world. The second world consisted of "the middle elements, such as Japan, Europe, Australia and Canada," who "do not possess so many atomic bombs and are not so rich as the First World, but richer than the Third World." The third world was Africa, Asia (without Japan) and Latin America—the people. Mao's economics were bad, but his sense of global strategy strong. China needed to peel off allies from the United States and the Soviet Union.

Awkward adjustments

The great Sino-American diplomatic shift was neither democratic nor participatory. This elite decision was made in secrecy from other nations and even policymakers in both China and the United States. While many Chinese and Americans welcomed the change, others were alarmed. All sides needed extended discussion to make this major ideological adjustment, as yesterday's archenemy became today's ally against the Soviet Union.

Japanese leaders, who had had been loyal supporters of the hard U.S. line in East Asia, were shocked to find the policy turned upside down without their consultation. The U.S. puppet government in South Vietnam knew that its end was near. Taiwan faced the news with stunned disbelief.

In U.S. domestic politics, outraged conservatives had always backed the Guomindang although Nixon managed to bring along most Republicans. America's intellectuals tried to explain the Chinese revolution, including some rather naïve analyses of the Cultural Revolution.

In China, the opening phase of the Cultural Revolution had reinvigorated an older xenophobia, sometimes by design and sometimes simply because the nation's most cosmopolitan voices were silenced. Yet the leftist Jiang Qing was committed to modernize China's culture by adapting Western techniques, very much in the spirit of Mao's call to "use the foreign to serve China." One model opera, *On the Docks*, showed Shanghai dockworkers struggling to export rice seeds to Africa, within a context of a global wave of anti-imperialism. This internationalism differed from importing Western cultural products, but it was not anti-foreign.

10. Jiang Qing entertains foreign guests on China's national day.

Even so, foreign culture was perhaps inevitably embroiled in bitter factional politics. An anxiety over contamination from abroad spread among many leftists, fearful of weakening the revolution by making China dependent upon foreign nations. More generously, leaders debated how to regulate the new opening to the West.

When Zhou Enlai organized a group of artists to decorate hotels for a new wave of foreign guests, radicals condemned the paintings as "black art." When Western classical music was once again performed, a campaign emerged to criticize "music without titles," because abstract symphonies and sonatas (e.g., Mozart's Symphony 40 in g minor) were seen as more bourgeois than title-bearing program music (Strauss's *Don Quixote* or Beethoven's *Pastoral Symphony*). Titled messages were seemingly more transparent, and they fit more comfortably within Chinese traditions of music and narrative. After a Chinese industrial delegation returned from a New York trip with a collection of glass snails presented to it by Corning Glass Works, Jiang Qing accused them of worshiping foreign things and demanded that they be returned. When the Italian film director Michelangelo Antonioni made a documentary to reintroduce China to the West, Beijing vilified him for focusing too often on old objects, quaint sights, and human-powered implements, instead of China's proud new industrial achievements.

The revival of connections to the West was not all trench warfare. China purchased significant imports, most notably a set of fertilizer factories to boost farm output. China welcomed the CIA to set up listening posts against a now-shared Soviet adversary. The cultural front, however, remained more public—and more sensitive.

Most controversies involved China receiving foreign culture. Less turmoil attended China's new cultural diplomacy, which was better organized and more focused. China maintained its ties with old friends, exporting revolutionary opera to Algeria and Albania, and the Ministry of Culture organized its highly skilled "Oriental

Song and Dance Troupe" to perform to Third World audiences. For Westerners, China turned over a new leaf, directing attention away from the chaos of the Cultural Revolution and toward the less politicized glories of China's past. The 1974 discovery of the "Terracotta Army" of thousands of warrior statues guarding the nearly two-thousand-year-old tomb of China's first emperor captured world attention, along with a traveling exhibition of archeological objects unearthed during the Cultural Revolution. Ironically, many of these had been discovered during the civil defense campaign to "dig tunnels deep, store grain everywhere."

China enlisted Westerners to present itself to the world. Han Suyin, a popular Sino-Belgian writer, introduced the People's Republic to new audiences. The New Zealand propagandist Rewi Alley turned out enthusiastic but mindless books and poems. Jiang Qing also found her own American biographer, Roxane Witke, a young academic who interviewed her extensively in 1972. Jiang Qing and Witke later both endured criticism for their cooperative project, although only Jiang was accused of betraying her nation.

Japan posed a special case, as China wooed its former enemy more ardently than in recent years. Chinese audiences thrilled to a Japanese dance troupe, which performed *The White-Haired Girl*. But haunting memories remained. A Japanese soldier, separated from his unit in the confused surrender in 1945, had settled in a North China village. Out of fear that Chinese peasants would seek vengeance, he blended into his community by pretending to be deaf and unable to speak. The restoration of relations between Japan and China revived his speech and hearing, and he returned home after three decades.

Groundwork for neoliberalism

What is the relationship between the Cultural Revolution and the resurgent China of our contemporary global economy? The conventional narrative maintains that the Cultural Revolution was the opposite of globalization, that a decade of xenophobic chaos and economic ruin was only put right when Deng Xiaoping wisely recognized reality and reintegrated China with the world economy.

The relationship to the reforms is more complex. The Cultural Revolution, especially in its early radical phase, marked a high point for zeal in resistance to global capitalism. Western triumphalists will obviously celebrate its defeat. Yet explaining changes in China simply as responses to the West remains inaccurate and narcissistic.

For all their blundering, Maoists built physical plant and human resources that were indispensible for subsequent rapid growth. Diminishing the contributions of the revolutionaries who dragged their nation into the modern world, ended illiteracy, combated chronic disease, and laid the infrastructure for industrialization is perverse. Despite the abundant shortcomings of Maoist China, the subsequent economic boom also builds upon its achievements, including national and social emancipation.

Although the Cultural Revolution could have done better for the economy, it is misleading to consider it merely a lost decade for China's development. China found greater international opportunities after the Cultural Revolution than before. The economic reintegration of China and world capitalism took place when the latter required China's vast labor reserves, which it did not in the smaller global economy of the mid-1960s.

Neoliberalism took shape in part as a reaction to resistance to world capitalism in the 1960s and 1970s. The turn to China's orderly, educated, and low-cost labor was ironic. Corporations in the United States, Europe, and Japan used offshore production in China to discipline workers back home with threats of job loss, as wages stagnated and labor unions weakened.

However much the reform program liberalized the economy, it remained a state-directed venture rather than a naïve opening of China's doors to capitalism. China's revolution, including the Cultural Revolution, formed a long-term movement to strengthen China to compete in the broader world. Hiring out its cheap labor supply to global capitalism was a calculated strategy, much like earlier Maoist efforts to harness these same workers through political campaigns.

China benefited mightily from the Vietnamese defeat of the United States. Americans were forced to recalculate their Asian strategy, creating the opening for Mao to ease China's isolation. Deng Xiaoping's post-Mao reforms were momentous but grew out of the Cultural Revolution policies of Mao, Zhou Enlai, and Deng himself. Through the end of the Cultural Revolution, détente with the United States permitted greater economic experimentation and a steady rise in foreign trade.

This is not to say that Mao knowingly steered China on the course it has pursued since his death. Mao was intensely apprehensive about capitalist representatives who had "sneaked" into positions of power, as he explained in the May 16 Notification that opened the Cultural Revolution: "Once conditions are ripe, they will seize political power and turn the dictatorship of the proletariat into a dictatorship of the bourgeoisie. Some of them we have already seen through; others we have not. Some are still trusted by us and are being trained as our successors, persons like Khrushchev for example, who are still nestling beside us."

One American academic and business consultant who visited China during the Cultural Revolution rode the train from Hong Kong with journalists from a radical U.S. magazine. He was gleeful when, upon arriving in China, the left-wing journalists were shepherded into a minibus, while he was driven off in a limousine, a precursor of change to come.

"We have friends all over the world": the Cultural Revolution's global context

99

For China, foreign investment demanded curbs on socialist institutions. "Self-reliance" sounds like more like Ronald Reagan or Margaret Thatcher than Mao. The slogan was dropped, but the concept was applied to individual Chinese workers. Agriculture was decollectivized by 1983. Soon after, some factories hired outsiders to perform the "voluntary" labor that the state had demanded, showing socialism's increasing hollowness. The "iron rice bowl" of lifetime employment, once regarded as an achievement of the worker's state, became an obstacle to competition in the world economy. The opening to foreign trade, privatization, and foreign investment produced a rapid growth in incomes. China became significantly less poor but also less equal and politically passive.

During the 2008 financial crisis, rumors circulated that the Chinese were going to rescue the bankrupt Lehman Brothers. The China once feared as the backer of revolution had become the China that made the world safe for global capitalism.

Thinking about the Cultural Revolution resembles the debate on climate change, where simple questions lead quickly to big and complicated issues. How should China reduce carbon emissions? The answer turns out to involve complex historical issues: the appropriate carbon load for early industrializers, the realistic ambitions of poorer nations, and the relationship of Chinese industrialization to such places as Africa. Similarly, the Cultural Revolution can certainly be discussed as a local issue of Chinese politics. But one wants also to understand how it fits with rest of world. We cannot understand China without considering its global context. And the world make little sense if we do not include China.

Chapter 6
Coming to terms with the Cultural Revolution

The Cultural Revolution began to wind down with Mao's death in 1976. Mao's widow and three other radical leaders were arrested as the "Gang of Four," blamed for the chaos, and put on public trial with Lin Biao's top generals in 1981. The arrests underscored the rising power of Deng Xiaoping and the gradual but systematic repudiation of most Maoist social and economic policies. Unsurprisingly, China has had a difficult time coping with the memory of such a traumatic period, although the country makes a more serious effort than many in the West will credit.

Ending the Cultural Revolution

In 1976, the ailing Mao Zedong reminisced about his achievements, including defeating Japan and victory in the civil war.

> The other thing, as you know, was to launch the Great Cultural Revolution. Here I don't have many supporters and I have quite a few opponents. The Great Cultural Revolution is something that has not yet been concluded. Thus I am passing the task on to the next generation. I may not be able to pass it on peacefully, in which case I may have to pass it on in turmoil. What will happen to the next generation if it all fails? There may be a foul wind and rain of blood. How will you cope? Heaven only knows!

Mao's anxieties about bloody rain were overstated. A simple coup against the faction most invested in continuing the Cultural Revolution assured its end. Most Party leaders agreed that the Cultural Revolution was politically destructive, that its economic policies had gone as far as they could, and that its cultural vision had become stifling.

Within a year of Ma's death, his successor, Hua Guofeng, declared that the Cultural Revolution was over. But Hua, one-time Hunan Party chief and minister of public security, needed to invoke Mao's heritage to strengthen his own weak political base. However, simultaneously invoking Mao while distancing himself from Mao's final heritage proved unmanageable. Hua was undone by the growing tide of rehabilitated officials who preferred the faster pace of change promised by Deng Xiaoping.

By December 1978, Deng had effectively stripped Hua of real authority. The Party embraced reform and began to reassess the Cultural Revolution more seriously. In the arts, a new "scar" literature exposed its injustices and corruption. Once-sacred Maoist models fell from grace. Critics revealed state subsidies to the "self-reliant" Dazhai production brigade as agricultural collectives were disbanded. Daqing ran out of oil, and its "petroleum faction" of politicos in Beijing was brought down when an offshore oil rig sank in 1979, killing seventy-two workers.

Shifts in social and cultural policy demonstrated the repudiation of the Cultural Revolution. Absent Maoist pressure, no one really wanted to keep city youth in the villages. By 1980 most had returned to their home cities. Nationwide college entrance examinations resumed. The age limit was raised to thirty-seven, to compensate for the decade of missed opportunity. Nearly 6 million people took what may have been history's most competitive examination; 5 percent won university places. This "Class of '77" is still regarded as a remarkable cohort.

Education and arts policies emphasized restoration of the old institutions and rehabilitation of purged officials, all in the spirit of recapturing an earlier imagined golden age of Chinese Communism but without Mao or Lin Biao. The 1980 memorial service for Liu Shaoqi accompanied a wave of rehabilitations, with honors for those who had died and compensation for those who had spent years in the political wilderness.

More subversive to Maoism, in the long run, were new economic initiatives to encourage markets and exports. Although China has a deep tradition of marketing, the revolution had destroyed its capitalist class. Among many ironies was former Red Guards using personal relations formed in Cultural Revolution politics to forge new business networks.

Cultural excitement increased with the rediscovery of styles and works from China's past and from the outside world. Artists and audiences rushed to make sense of a sudden profusion of aesthetic choice. Resistance flared on and off from more conservative (not necessarily Maoist) officials, frequently centered around imported popular music, including Theresa Teng, a sensuous Taiwan singer. Deng Xiaoping put it more calmly than some anxious lower officials: "When you open the window, some flies will get in."

Most censorship was enforced by the zealous or the fearful, and it began to ease. New historical perspectives permitted a more nuanced discussion of China's past, so that 1949 no longer marked the dividing line between good and bad. A rediscovery of Republican China was at last detached from military threats from Chiang Kai-shek.

Assigning responsibility

It is not true that Chinese authorities have never come to grips with the Cultural Revolution. Westerners remain generally unaware of the extent of Communist Party apology, renunciation, and compensation for this Maoist movement, including public trials, rehabilitations of victims, and restorations of jobs, lost property, and income.

In 1981 the Chinese Communist Party Central Committee passed a resolution on Party history, which included a clear repudiation of the Cultural Revolution. "The 'Cultural Revolution,' which lasted from May 1966 to October 1976, was responsible for the most severe setback and the heaviest losses suffered by the Party, the state, and people since the founding of the People Republic. It was initiated and led by Comrade Mao Zedong."

The resolution continued: "Practice has shown that the 'Cultural Revolution' did not in fact constitute a revolution or social progress in any sense, nor could it possibly have done so. It was we and not the enemy at all who were thrown into disorder by the 'Cultural Revolution.'"

The televised public trial of members of Gang of Four and the Lin Biao Clique in 1980 offered some symbolic closure for millions of fascinated viewers. The ten defendants stood accused of persecuting 727,420 people and killing 34,274. Jiang Qing spoke defiantly. Shanghai's Zhang Chunqiao (perhaps the most serious political leader among the defendants) refused to speak at all. Both were sentenced to death, with a two-year suspension, later altered to life imprisonment. Former Party vice-chairman Wang Hongwen received a life sentence, and the fallen propagandist Yao Wenyuan got twenty years. Chen Boda, Mao's onetime secretary and leader of the Cultural Revolution Group, and the top military leaders who were condemned as "Lin Biao faction members" were sentenced to between sixteen and eighteen years.

Jiang Qing remained a political prisoner until her suicide in 1991. Perhaps in the spirit of the new export-oriented economy, she made dolls for sale abroad. This assignment was cancelled when jailers discovered that she embroidered her name on each doll.

The Party posthumously expelled Kang Sheng and Xie Fuzhi, deceased leaders of the security system; even the eulogies delivered at their funerals were officially rescinded. Massive purges at the local level accompanied suicides of some leftist activists. The trial of the Gang of Four signaled a second round of local purges, including people who had been Red Guard activists nearly two decades before, as well as late Cultural Revolution "heroes" such as university exam critic Zhang Tiesheng, who received fifteen years for subversion.

Many once-vanquished officials were returned to high office, sometimes only in honorific roles, sometimes with vengeance on their minds. Many were rewarded with foreign travel. Less formally, their children often received preference in promotions. As more general public symbolism, a new design for China's paper currency added a bespectacled intellectual to the Maoist trio of a worker, peasant, and soldier, making official the renewed respect for intellectuals.

The state returned much property confiscated during the Cultural Revolution. By 1985, the Beijing Cultural Relics Bureau "Office for Goods Ransacked During the Cultural Revolution" put 30,000 unclaimed art works and 170,000 books on display, so that citizens might file claims for their return. Unsurprisingly, some of the most desirable items attracted multiple claims.

Yet critics wanted more. Why criticize the Cultural Revolution but not the Great Leap Forward? Others wanted a Party renunciation of the anti-rightist campaign of 1957. Still others wished for a renunciation of the revolution itself. Party and state leaders could not satisfy all of China's citizens, who ranged from workers whose lives had improved to intellectuals who had suffered bitterly. In the end, China dealt with its controversial past, as other societies have done—with frustrating limits.

Within these limits, the signals were clear. The Party positioned itself rather defensively, shifting as much blame as possible to

Mao and the Gang of Four, then urging everyone to "look to the future." Yet if we include as victims of the Cultural Revolution anyone with an ill-treated family member, perhaps 100 million Chinese suffered harm. As ever more purged officials enjoyed political rehabilitation and restoration of their former posts, many found themselves tensely sharing offices with their former accusers. Looking to the future became all the more urgent but nearly impossible.

The Party began desacralizing Maoism. Mao had been buried, with some controversy, in an enormous mausoleum at the center of Beijing's Tiananmen Square. Rather than dismantle the tomb, the Party opted to expand the memorial to include five other Communist leaders: Liu Shaoqi, Zhu De, Zhou Enlai, Chen Yun, (and later) Deng Xiaoping. Mao's *Collected Works* continued to be published in four volumes, which included his writings through the 1949 revolution. A newer volume 5, composed of essays written between 1949 and 1976, seemed too radical and was withdrawn.

Hundreds of no-longer-fashionable statues of Mao were dismantled. Many had stood on university campuses, where they were especially unpopular. At Beijing University at the end of 1987, a professor displayed pieces of a shattered statue in his office. Much like other Chinese hosts offer tea, fruit, or cigarettes to guests, the professor welcomed visitors by handing out pieces of Mao. A dismembered Mao symbolized the new courage of China's intellectuals, and their victory over a once-commanding and sometimes menacing presence.

The Party's reaction against Mao included removing the "four big rights" from the national constitution in 1980. Speaking out freely, airing views fully, holding great debates, and writing big-character posters disappeared as rights (along with the right to strike). Party veterans saw those provisions as encouragement to their critics.

Moreover, the four big rights had just been invoked in the popular 1979 demonstrations at Beijing's Democracy Wall.

But Deng and his followers could not be certain of control; the demonstrators included former Red Guards, recently returned from the countryside and hungry for both jobs and political reforms. Their big character posters especially frightened leaders with unpleasant memories of past denunciations. They happily used the crisis to end mass political movements, perhaps the most central Maoist political legacy. Yet in their way, the four big rights also protected freedom of expression against authority. Western governments looked the other way, either to support Deng's new regime or because they could not imagine a Maoist heritage with positive implications for human rights.

Books and articles about the Cultural Revolution included memoirs and joke books. Both genres typically aimed to reestablish the damaged social position of intellectuals. Cultural Revolution jokes included the worker put in charge of an arts center who, when rain ruined the darkroom, developed the film out of doors. Or a worker made into a librarian classified the popular Russian novel *How the Steel Was Tempered* under the heading of metallurgy.

But constraints slowed the movement to criticize Mao and the Cultural Revolution. First, as the Party reconsolidated its authority, it still relied on Mao's heritage for legitimacy. Mao was said to be 70 percent good and 30 percent bad, an ambiguous formula that left much unspecified. Second, the Cultural Revolution had reached out to embrace hundreds of millions of ordinary citizens. These working people sought to live up to the movement's ideals in their daily lives, often in spite of the machinations of the political elite. The Party could not denounce the Chinese people, whose fundamental wisdom and goodness it was required to defend.

The 1989 upheaval and Cultural Revolution nostalgia

Party uncertainties were firmed up in China's great 1989 political crisis. Massive popular demonstrations originally protested corruption and inflation, then expanded to calls for greater democracy. Many of the marchers were Party members. This great social movement sparked demonstrations throughout China until its violent suppression on June 4. The demonstrations split the Communist Party, whose general gecretary, Zhao Ziyang, was dismissed and placed under house arrest until his death in 2005.

The victorious faction of the Party deployed memories of the Cultural Revolution to discredit its new critics. For example, Zhang Hua's remorseful essay, "Report on Destroying Books" (see chap. 3) was published on April 18, 1989, two days before martial law was imposed on Beijing. Through such reminiscences the Party tapped into a very real anxiety about social disorder. The specter of the Cultural Revolution haunted the Party establishment, which had regained its reputation and power only a decade earlier. It also haunted the youthful demonstrators, who had to guard against the charge that they were merely reviving Red Guard hooliganism.

The demonstrators sharply distinguished themselves from Red Guards by their discipline, unity, and modesty. As in the Cultural Revolution, students were in the foreground of the movement. But in 1989 they presented themselves not as rebels but as students, the nation's future elite, patriotically concerned about China's course. Yet inevitably the new demonstrators of 1989 drew upon the repertory of politics for collective action, which they shared with the Red Guard generation. Deng suppressed his critics with violence, then demonized them in national propaganda, reacting somewhat like China's panicked political elite of 1968, when the Red Guards were closed down.

After the Beijing massacre of June 4 the Party reestablished its political grip, then lightened up on public treatment of the Cultural Revolution in an unprecedented wave of happy-faced nostalgia. Cultural Revolution restaurants sprang up, serving food that recalled time spent in the countryside, though with a lot more meat for newly prosperous former Red Guards. Cultural Revolution artifacts became popular collectibles, including Mao badges, posters, and statues. Dramas once patronized by Jiang Qing were performed before enthusiastic audiences, and Maoist songs were set to a disco beat.

This Mao fever of early 1990s accompanied a profound deepening of economic reform, as Deng encouraged citizens to "leap into the sea" of the market to jump-start an economy made stagnant by the 1989 violence. The "Mao fever" was mere nostalgia, lacking any Maoist political message. The Cultural Revolution was marketed for the new reform era, just as almost everything else in Chinese culture was becoming a commodity. Mao fever resembles Western pop culture nostalgia for 1960s—wild colors, lots of hair, spiritual explorations, and zany beliefs, but marked omission of now-awkward struggles against racism, poverty, or imperialist war.

A popular film, *In the Heat of the Sun* (1994), explored the Cultural Revolution through the story of a fifteen-year-old left home alone by his military officer family to explore Beijing in 1975. His coming-of-age adventures examined the thrill of a young man without adult supervision, including participating in gang fights, exploring sex, savoring food, and discovering adult hypocrisy. This wistful nostalgia was in sharp contrast to the grim June 4 suppression.

An expanding cultural marketplace meant that propaganda officials struggled to regulate discussion of the Cultural Revolution. The topic was never banned outright but in fact stimulated many books and lots of art. Yet in 1990 the Propaganda Department blocked a proposed dictionary of the Cultural

11. Cultural Revolution–inspired imagery now often appears as irony. The People's Sandwich of Portland offers a fine Hammer and Pickle sandwich.

Revolution. This project was deemed far too serious and might reopen old controversies while defining old words and phrases. But similar projects were completed, reflecting an effort to comprehend China's recent tumultuous past.

Treatment of the Cultural Revolution understandably remains a political minefield. The risks are now intensified by the Party's own contradictory attitudes. For example, a biography of the former minister of culture Yu Huiyong, a composer who worked on revolutionary operas, was withdrawn from circulation in 1994 because it was too "objective." The leadership was not ready for dispassionate discussion that did not vilify its old enemies. Yet this stance ran counter to commercialized nostalgia, which kept the model operas in performance. The commercial economy guarantees that the nostalgia market for 1960s music will be exploited, yet the stern and unyielding political verdict on the movement means that serious inquiry risks painful controversy.

A discomfiting heritage

China is hardly unusual in dealing with a controversial past. Memories of radical political movements are especially tricky when high-minded goals join violent politics. The United States has never been comfortable with the figure of the abolitionist John Brown, hanged for leading an armed rebellion against slavery. Russians lack an easy consensus on the Bolsheviks. Unlike China's Cultural Revolution, neither of these examples includes the emotions of still-living participants.

The Cultural Revolution generation appears as distinctively tough to many Chinese, trained by difficult experiences to be politically savvy and personally determined. Because the era was cynical, calculating, and brutal, both former Red Guards and their victims take pride in their personal strength. The dissident artist Ai Weiwei is the son of poet Ai Qing, a veteran revolutionary who fell afoul of the Party leadership, much like Ai Weiwei in 2011. Despite Ai Qing's personal relationship to Mao Zedong, Ai Weiwei recalls that his father was demoted to cleaning toilets. "They were broken public toilets, dirty and messy. Sometimes he would come home covered in shit. He didn't have extra clothes. But he was calm and he said: 'For sixty years I didn't know who cleaned my toilet.' That was so convincing for us."

But reminiscences of personal discoveries and defeats seldom enter public discourse. Indeed, they often remain unmentioned within families. One intellectual couple who shared dinner with a foreigner in 1989 astonished their twelve-year-old son by mentioning that his parents had met as Red Guards. Yet the couple believe that the post–Cultural Revolution generation is spoiled, lacking firsthand experience with China's problems. The Red Guard generation has come to power within Chinese institutions, but the nation has still not opened up to discussion of the broad range of its experiences. Though it is untrue to say that the topic is closed, the conversation has largely been channeled into an unsatisfying hash of nostalgia, ignorance, and guilt.

Nearly half a century after the Cultural Revolution began, persecutors and victims alike have died or retired. The current political leadership avoids poking around in the increasingly ancient youthful politics of today's elite. But why would this stir up more trouble than questions about which U.S. leaders fought in Vietnam, and who dodged the draft?

China's leadership yearns to keep tactics of mass mobilization out of politics. This strategy no doubt helps keep the lid on Cultural Revolution discussions. Surprisingly boisterous social protests rage across China, anchored firmly in the tensions of the economic reform era. Among recent protesters, including state workers, home-losers, pensioners, migrants, and the unemployed, Mao's image has a persistent appeal. The Party wants to discourage them from Cultural Revolutionary thinking and responses. No restrictions bar former rusticated youth from arranging informal reunions and activities, but there have been impediments to more formal, organized behavior.

Another discouragement for discussing the Cultural Revolution is that top leaders likely disagree in their perspectives. Their personal and family experiences, as well as the feelings of their constituents would make a unity of views improbable. Better not to discuss it than to disagree.

This reticence replicates the Party's anxiety about public discussion of any big disasters, including the 1957 Anti-Rightist movement, the 1958 Great Leap Forward, and the 1989 Beijing massacre. Certain Cultural Revolution issues turn out to be acceptable, but no one knows which ones will be off limits. Cautious people to turn to other topics. There is something unstable about allowing criticism of Mao Zedong but ignoring demands for public memorials or museums dedicated to the Cultural Revolution. The novelist Ba Jin, for example, backed a museum project but got nowhere.

Interpretations of the Cultural Revolution have not remained stagnant but instead have evolved in response to broader political imperatives. A new interest appears, for instance, in the nature of sexuality during the Cultural Revolution decade, as aging Red Guards look back upon their golden youth, like baby boomers in the United States. Sexuality also poses fewer political issues than, say, reconsidering the role of the army, or Deng Xiaoping, or the experiences of current leaders. China's liberalization moves along the edges of society but only slowly alters the central institutions and myths.

Personal recriminations continue. Elderly intellectuals still attack one another for ratting out their friends. Depressing as these memories and exposés seem, they feed a public fascination with the dirty laundry of once-prominent figures.

As the commercialized economy has expanded, people who own intellectual "content" find new opportunities. Disputes have erupted over who now has rights to Cultural Revolutionary art, which was often created under collective auspices. The *Rent Collection Courtyard*, a hundred-figure sculpture of a Sichuan landlord mistreating his peasants, was a 1960s tourist mecca; a parody by Cai Guoqiang featured at the 2000 Venice Biennale; surviving sculptors of the 1960s sued their nonrevolutionary successors for refusing to honor their rights. The heirs of composer Li Jiefu, who set Mao's words to song, sought compensation when the Mao fever of the 1990s recycled his music. A long court battle blew up over the rights to the oil painting *Chairman Mao on His Way to Anyuan* by Liu Chunhua (1968). In 1995 Liu sold the painting to a bank, which now still owns it despite claims by the National Museum in Beijing and state recognition of the work as a cultural relic.

Lei Feng, the model Maoist soldier, remains alive and respected in the public imagination. But he is not so respected as in the Cultural Revolution. The introduction of Lei Feng brand condoms scandalized many, and the brand was removed from sale in 2007. Two years later an actor selected to portray Lei Feng in a television series had to dodge charges that his private escapades disqualified him from such an exalted role.

The oddly constrained channels for discussion heighten the Cultural Revolution's appeal as satire. Yan Lianke's 2005 novel, *Serve the People*, describes a torrid affair between a wife of a Maoist military commander and his servant. Their passions soar as they destroy revolutionary symbols, including writings and statues of Mao, thereby mingling sexual and political transgressions. The novel was published in a leading literary magazine, although the book version was blocked. Yan, who was eight years old in 1966, is a prizewinning author whose career seems not to have suffered, and who no doubt enjoys the royalties from his foreign sales.

The future of the Cultural Revolution

The Cultural Revolution is dead and mostly buried, so dead that efforts to understand it risk being misunderstood as either whitewashing or failure to show sufficient indignation toward the corpse. Nonetheless, ideas about the Cultural Revolution will be part of our political and intellectual landscape for some time to come.

Inside China, the young show no great interest. Current leaders are no longer driven by the personal animus shared by the Deng Xiaoping generation. Time's passage will likely reduce the scale of Cultural Revolutionary memories, make it seem less an unparalleled explosion, and ground it more firmly within a century of turbulent change.

Some hints of this diminution of the Cultural Revolution have appeared, as the velocity of social change since Mao's death dominates popular consciousness. Chinese who have come of age in the reform era can learn more about the world than their 1960s counterparts, express wider views, and suffer less from a combination of Party bullying and lynch-mob activism. As individual victims pass from the scene, interest in rectifying or memorializing their cases abates. Other scandals, which once sparked great horror, such as the political destruction of traditional culture, have now been surpassed by later market-driven destruction. Whole neighborhoods are torn down by real estate speculators. Surviving practitioners of ancient arts are left almost without audiences. Similarly, Maoist environmental damage through poorly considered mass campaigns, shocking as it was, has been trumped by nearly unregulated expansion of private cars and polluting industries.

The Cultural Revolution heritage of paranoia, opportunism, and the destruction of values remains. But the earlier moral critique of the Cultural Revolution has been diminished by subsequent developments. Some said that Mao was responsible for the increase in bad manners, but the post–Cultural Revolution era reveals plenty of anomie, crime, and public thuggishness. The rising prosperity of the past three decades has also brought problems of social disintegration, environmental disaster, a growing gap between rich and poor, uneven economic development, ethnic conflict, and a widely held belief that China's social fabric is under great stress.

The raw harshness of the reform era sometimes elicits a nostalgia for Maoism that romanticizes the Cultural Revolution, contrasting Maoist concern for the public good and law and order with recent greed and corruption. The Party, now led by the kinds of politicians Mao warned against, is eager to keep Cultural Revolutionary analyses and methods out of labor disputes. Maoist appeals to workers were handled roughly in 2010 in Henan province, a traditional bastion of leftist thinking. Memory of the Cultural Revolution serves as a boogeyman to silence protests about a society that still faces severe contradictions. In this way the Cultural Revolution helps elite investors maintain order. Party anxieties are sharpest when economic growth is threatened, reminding us that the image of the Cultural Revolution is used not just against mass participation in public life but ultimately against democracy.

Yet the Cultural Revolution generation now runs China, not just in politics but in business, culture, and the military. Despite these leaders' often bitter experiences and disillusionments, many continue to be influenced by the idealism that inspired them as Red Guards. This desire for social justice, along with the realities of politics, fuels a continuing frustration that recent growth has left so many rural people left behind.

Less idealistically, Maoism reappears in interesting places. Classes on business strategy teach young entrepreneurs the Chairman's writings on revolution, advising them to surround major markets from minor cities, adding a capitalist twist to Mao's theory of revolution from the countryside against the cities. The Cultural Revolution plays little role in this curriculum. But Mao's appeal even to the business elite reminds us that Chinese nationalism is not going to jettison the Mao who was the patriot and nation-builder. China is stuck with Mao, for better or worse, as more dilemmas arise about how to deal with the Cultural Revolution.

Beyond China, the West has yet to come to terms with the Cultural Revolution. As the West wrestles with China's rise in the international community, the Cultural Revolution remains a useful and perhaps irresistible propaganda point. An imagined Western moral superiority is clarified by a typical and mistaken Cultural Revolution narrative: the economy was a shambles, education destroyed, but Deng Xiaoping rescued China by copying *our* free market. Kicking Mao's corpse strengthens the position of globalism, proves that socialism does not work, and reveals China as unstable and dangerous. If Mao survives as a nationalist symbol for China, so much the worse for China.

Western reporters sometimes quickly identify almost anyone of a certain age as a "Cultural Revolution survivor." "Survivor" embraces everyone, from people who endured truly hair-raising ordeals to many who were merely getting along with daily life. Everyone becomes a victim, which is true enough in the broadest terms. But the victim narrative ignores that some were more victimized than others and disregards the many varieties of suffering. It feeds a myth of holocaust and valorizes a Western self-perception as China's saviors.

This hoary trope from missionary times has risen again, strengthened by an influential series of memoirs from recent exiles. Typically a youth from a privileged family gets caught in a Maoist storm but is rescued by a scholarship to a Western university. The trajectory moves from a life in a bleak China, which the young Chinese was too naïve to recognize as totalitarian. The passions of the Cultural Revolution explode, sometimes accompanied by self-discovery, followed by a flight (never so identified) to the West. These memoirs are often very informative, well-written, and beloved by many readers. Their very talented, hard-working, and ambitious writers skillfully achieve a difficult connection with Western audiences. But these memoirs subtly flatter Western readers' sense of superiority as they oversimplify China.

Recurring assertions that China has failed to come to terms with the Cultural Revolution are not helpful. This uncompassionate judgment trivializes the difficulties any complex society faces when dealing with unpleasant parts of its past. One might argue that China has done about as well in facing the Cultural Revolution as the United States has with its invasion of Vietnam. Adorning the national currency with the face of Mao Zedong surely offends many, but so does naming the headquarters of the Federal Bureau of Investigation the J. Edgar Hoover Building.

China continues to intrigue the West. Foreign fascination with China during the Cultural Revolution was often naïve, but it did mark a turn in which Westerners began seriously considering political ideas from Asia. The Cultural Revolution was also the point of China's greatest ideological distance from the West, which magnified (and blurred) the allure of a possible alterative modernity, apparently free from colonialism and capitalism. Contemporary discussion of China also sees an alternative to the West, this time not Maoist but vaguely Confucian, and as an unexpected economic rival. The West now regards China with utter seriousness, and the beguilement of the 1960s has turned into an unsettled mix of fear, indignation, and financial opportunism.

Timeline

1905	Abolition of the Confucian Imperial Examination system.
1911	Collapse of Qing Dynasty; overthrow of emperor and establishment of Republic.
1919	May Fourth movement to modernize culture and politics begins with demonstrations against Treaty of Versailles, which handed German rights in Shandong province to Japan.
1921	Founding of Chinese Communist Party.
1927	Chiang Kai-shek purges Communist allies.
1931	Japan invades China's Manchurian provinces.
1934–35	Long March of Communists to retreat from Guomindang attack.
1937–45	War of Resistance against Japan.
1942	Yan'an Rectification: Mao consolidates position in Communist Party through intellectual remolding of intellectuals to serve workers, peasants, and soldiers.
1949	Establishment of the People's Republic of China; Guomindang government flees to Taiwan.
1950	Marriage Law bans polygamy and arranged marriages; land reform.
1950–53	China and United States fight to standoff in Korean War.
1953–57	First Five-Year Plan institutionalizes Soviet model of planned collective economy.

1956-57	"Hundred Flowers" campaign enlists critical support of non-Party intellectuals.
1957-58	Anti-Rightist Campaign silences critical intellectuals.
1958	Great Leap Forward.
1959-61	Collapse of Great Leap Forward; famine.
1960	Soviet Union recalls technical advisors from China.
1962	Market experiments; Mao: "Never Forget Class Struggle."
1963	Study Lei Feng Campaign.
1964	China tests first nuclear bomb; Third Front construction project begins.
1966	Cultural Revolution begins. Mass rallies of Red Guards.
1967	Efforts to reconstitute local power by forcing political alliances.
1968	Red Guards sent to countryside; end of radical phase of Cultural Revolution.
1969	Border clashes with Soviet Union; Ninth Party Congress. Lin Biao named as Mao's successor.
1970	China puts first satellite in orbit.
1971	Lin Biao dies in Outer Mongolia plane crash. China regains United Nations seat.
1972	U.S. President Richard Nixon visits China. Normalization between United States and China begins.
1973	Deng Xiaoping is restored to power.
1974	"Criticize Lin Biao and Confucius" campaign to protect Cultural Revolution.
1975	Second purge of Deng Xiaoping.
1976	Premier Zhou Enlai dies; Tiananmen Square demonstrations; Tangshan earthquake. Mao Zedong dies; armed forces arrest Jiang Qing and her associates, labeled as Gang of Four.
1977	National university entrance examination restored.
1978	Deng Xiaoping introduces market-oriented economic reforms.
1979	Democracy Wall; establishment of diplomatic relations between the United States and China.

1980-81	Trial of Gang of Four and Lin Biao counterrevolutionary cliques.
1989	Nationwide demonstrations for political reform, ended by Beijing Massacre.
1991	Jiang Qing commits suicide in prison.
1992	Deng Xiaoping expands market reforms.

Timeline

Major actors in the Cultural Revolution

Bo Yibo (1908–2007). Head of State Planning Commission and an early Cultural Revolution target.

Chen Boda (1904–89). A leading Party propagandist as editor of *Red Flag* magazine, Chen became chair of the Cultural Revolution Group in 1966. When the radical phase of the Cultural Revolution ended, Chen lost influence. He was tried with the Gang of Four and members of the Lin Biao clique.

Deng Xiaoping (1904–97). Party secretary-general in 1966 damned as the "number two person in authority taking the capitalist road." Nonetheless respected by Mao for his political ability, he was called back to work as deputy prime minister in 1973 but purged again in 1976. China's "paramount leader" (that is, without holding a top office) from 1978 to 1996 and chief architect of post-Mao reforms and of violent suppression of 1989 political unrest.

Hua Guofeng (1921–2008). Provincial politician in Hunan, promoted during Cultural Revolution in wake of Lin Biao affair. After Zhou Enlai's death, Hua became the second prime minister of the People's Republic and succeeded Mao as Party chairman. Hua was instrumental in arrest of Gang of Four, but was politically outmaneuvered by Deng Xiaoping, giving up his chief posts in 1980–81, although he retained membership in the Party central committee until 2002.

Jiang Qing (1914–91). Originally an actress, Jiang Qing became Mao's third wife in 1938. Mao's colleagues barred her from politics by a prenuptial agreement. She became an important ally to her husband during the Cultural Revolution.

Kang Sheng (1898–1975). Veteran Party leader overseeing Party internal security, and thus a key ally for Mao in the Cultural Revolution.

Lin Biao (1907–1971). Celebrated Communist military leader who radicalized the army in the years leading to the Cultural Revolution. Once Mao's "closest comrade in arms" and designated successor, Lin became embroiled in a still-murky plot, ending in the crash of his plane in Outer Mongolia.

Liu Shaoqi (1898–1969). Organizer of Communist underground resistance during revolution, and president of China 1959–68. Mao's presumed successor, but as "China's Khrushchev," the major target of the Cultural Revolution.

Mao Zedong (1893–1976). Leader of Communist Party 1935–76. Chinese president 1954–59. Organizer of Cultural Revolution.

Peng Zhen (1902–97). Beijing city Party leader and early target of Maoist wrath for blocking leftist policies. Rehabilitated to become a leader of the National People's Congress in the 1980s.

Wang Hongwen (1935–92). Youngest member of the Gang of Four. Korean war veteran who rose from security work in a Shanghai factory to join national politics during the Cultural Revolution.

Yao Wenyuan (1931–2005). Shanghai journalist and literary critic. His critique of a play by a Beijing vice-mayor helped Mao to initiate his attack on the Beijing leadership. Yao was promoted to the center but may have been the lightweight of the Gang of Four.

Zhang Chunqiao (1917–2005). Party intellectual who rose to power in Cultural Revolution takeover of Shanghai government. Promoted to central Party organization, arrested after Mao's death. Zhang was the most theoretically minded of the Gang of Four.

References

Chapter 1

Mao's remarks to Malraux appear in André Malraux, *Anti-Memoirs* (New York: Holt, Rinehart, and Winston, 1968), 373–74, 373. They may be as much Malraux as Mao, but the spirit is correct.

Chapter 2

Michael Schoenhals and Roderick MacFarquhar trace the movement's political currents in *Mao's Last Revolution* (Cambridge, MA: Harvard University Press, 2006). On Red Guards, see Andrew G. Walder, *Fractured Rebellion: The Beijing Red Guard Movement* (Cambridge, MA: Harvard University Press, 2009). Frederick Teiwes and Warren Sun deconstruct *The End of the Maoist Era: Chinese Politics during the Twilight of the Cultural Revolution, 1972–1976* (Armonk, NY: M. E. Sharpe, 2007). For the role of urban workers, see Elizabeth Perry and Li Xun, *Proletarian Power: Shanghai in the Cultural Revolution* (Boulder, CO: Westview Press, 2000). Jiang Yang describes the rural exile of urban intellectuals in *A Cadre School Life: Six Chapters* (Hong Kong: Joint Publication Company, 1982).

Chapter 3

Paul Clark surveys the radical arts program in *The Chinese Cultural Revolution: A History* (Cambridge: Cambridge University Press, 2008).

Chapter 4

See Barry Naughton, *The Chinese Economy. Transitions and Growth* (Cambridge, MA: MIT Press, 2007); and Chris Bramall, *Chinese Economic Development* (London: Routledge, 2009). For contrarian views of rural life, see Gao Mobo, *Gao Village* (Honolulu: University of Hawaii Press, 1999).

Chapter 5

On the international implications of the Cultural Revolution, see Ma Jisen, *The Cultural Revolution in the Foreign Ministry of China* (Hong Kong: Chinese University Press, 2004); and Anne-Marie Brady, *Making the Foreign Serve China: Managing Foreigners in the People's Republic* (Lanham, MD: Rowman and Littlefield, 2003).

Mao's anxiety about capitalist-roaders is quoted in Schoenhals and MacFarquhar, 47.

Chapter 6

Mao's comments on the end of the Cultural Revolution are found in Michael Schoenhals, *China's Cultural Revolution: Not a Dinner Party* (Armonk, NY: M. E. Sharpe, 1996), 293.

For Ai Qing and the toilets, see David Pilling, "Lunch with the FT: Ai Weiwei," *Financial Times*, April 23, 2010.

Geremie R. Barmé explores Mao in the post–Cultural Revolutionary popular imagination in *Shades of Mao: The Posthumous Cult of the Great Leader* (Armonk, NY: M. E. Sharpe, 1996).

Further reading

Barmé, Geremie R. *Shades of Mao: The Posthumous Cult of the Great Leader*. Armonk, NY: M. E. Sharpe, 1996.

Baum, Richard. *Burying Mao: Chinese Politics in the Age of Deng Xiaoping*. Princeton, NJ: Princeton University Press, 1994.

Bramall, Chris. *Chinese Economic Development*. London: Routledge, 2009.

Brady, Anne-Marie. *Making the Foreign Serve China: Managing Foreigners in the People's Republic*. Lanham, MD: Rowman and Littlefield, 2003.

Chan, Anita, Richard Madsen, and JonathanUnger. *Chen Village: The Recent History of a Peasant Community in Mao's China*. Berkeley: University of California Press, 1984.

Chang, Jung. *Wild Swans: Three Daughters of China*. New York: Simon and Schuster, 1991.

Cheng, Nien. *Life and Death in Shanghai*. New York: Grove, 1987.

Clark, Paul. *The Chinese Cultural Revolution: A History*. Cambridge: Cambridge University Press, 2008.

Esherick, Joseph W., Paul G. Pickowicz, and Andrew G. Walder, eds. *The Chinese Cultural Revolution as History*. Stanford, CA: Stanford University Press, 2006.

Gao Mobo. *Gao Village*. Honolulu: University of Hawaii Press, 1999.

Gao Yuan. *Born Red: A Chronicle of the Cultural Revolution*. Stanford, CA: Stanford University Press, 1987.

Goldstein, Melvyn, Ben Jiao, and Tanzen Lhundrup. *On the Cultural Revolution in Tibet: The Nyemo Incident of 1969*. Berkeley: University of California Press, 2009.

Han, Dongping. *The Unknown Cultural Revolution*. New York: Monthly Review Press, 2008.

Jiang Yang. *A Cadre School Life: Six Chapters*. Hong Kong: Joint Publication Company, 1982.

Joseph, William A., Christine P. W. Wong, and David Zweig, eds. *New Perspectives on the Cultural Revolution*. Cambridge, MA: Harvard University Press, 1991.

Kraus, Richard Curt. *Pianos and Politics in China: Middle-Class Ambitions and the Struggle over Western Music*. New York: Oxford University Press, 1989.

Law, Kam-yee. *The Chinese Cultural Revolution Reconsidered: Beyond Purge and Holocaust*. Houndmills, UK: Palgrave Macmillan, 2003.

Lee, Ching Kwan, and Guobin Yang, eds. *Re-envisioning the Chinese Revolution: The Politics and Poetics of Collective Memories in Contemporary China*. Washington, DC: Woodrow Wilson Center Press and Stanford University Press, 2007.

Li Zhensheng. *Red-Color News Soldier: Photographs of the Cultural Revolution*. New York: Phaidon Press, 2003.

Li Zhisui. *The Private Life of Chairman Mao*. New York: Random House, 1994.

Liang Heng, and Judith Shapiro, *Son of the Revolution*. New York: Knopf, 1983.

Ma Jisen. *The Cultural Revolution in the Foreign Ministry of China*. Hong Kong: Chinese University Press, 2004.

Meisner, Maurice. *Mao's China and After: A History of the People's Republic*. New York: Free Press, 1986.

Milton, David, and Nancy Dall Milton. *The Wind Will Not Subside: Years in Revolutionary China*. New York: Pantheon, 1976.

Min, Anchee. *Red Azalea*. New York: Pantheon, 1994.

Mitter, Rana. *A Bitter Revolution: China's Struggle with the Modern World*. Oxford: Oxford University Press, 2004.

Naughton, Barry. *The Chinese Economy: Transitions and Growth*. Cambridge, MA: MIT Press, 2007.

Perry, Elizabeth, and Li Xun. *Proletarian Power: Shanghai in the Cultural Revolution*. Boulder, CO: Westview Press, 2000.

Rae Yang. *Spider Eaters: A Memoir*. Berkeley: University of California Press, 1997.

Riskin, Carl *China's Political Economy: The Quest for Development since 1949*. Oxford: Oxford University Press, 1987.

Schoenhals, Michael. *China's Cultural Revolution, 1966–1969: Not a Dinner Party*. Armonk, NY: M. E. Sharpe, 1996.

Schoenhals, Michael, and Roderick MacFarquhar. *Mao's Last Revolution*. Cambridge, MA: Harvard University Press, 2006.

Spence, Jonathan. *The Search for Modern China*. New York: Norton, 1990.

Teiwes, Frederick C., and Warren Sun. *The End of the Maoist Era: Chinese Politics during the Twilight of the Cultural Revolution, 1972–1976*. Armonk, NY: M. E. Sharpe, 2007.

Walder, Andrew G. *Fractured Rebellion: The Beijing Red Guard Movement*. Cambridge, MA: Harvard University Press, 2009.

Wang Ban, ed. *Words and Their Stories: Essays on the Language of the Chinese Revolution*. Leiden: Brill, 2010.

White, Lynn T. III. *Policies of Chaos: The Organizational Causes of Violence in China's Cultural Revolution*. Princeton, NJ: Princeton University Press, 1989.

Woei Lien Chong, ed. *China's Great Proletarian Cultural Revolution*. Lanham, MD: Rowman and Littlefield, 2002.

Yan Jiaqi, and Gao Gao. *Turbulent Decade: A History of the Cultural Revolution*. Honolulu: University of Hawai'i Press, 1996.

Yue Daiyun, and Carolyn Wakeman. *To the Storm: The Odyssey of a Revolutionary Chinese Woman*. Berkeley: University of California Press, 1985.

Websites

Morning Sun: A Film and Website about Cultural Revolution
www.morningsun.org
Videos, photos, and interviews related to the documentary film of the same title, from the Long Bow Group.

Chinese Posters: Propaganda, Politics, History, Art
chineseposters.net
Posters from the collections of International Institute of Social History, Amsterdam, and Stefan R. Landsberger.

Index

Index